OVERCOMING LIMITING BELIEFS

HOW TO REWIRE YOUR BRAIN, STOP OVERTHINKING, DEVELOP MENTAL TOUGHNESS, AND CHANGE YOUR PERSONALITY FOR GOOD

LUNA A. MAY

CONTENTS

1

BREAKING FREE

Have you ever found yourself paralyzed by self-doubt? An opportunity or aspiration surfaces, but instead of charging forward, you feel a shroud of fear and uncertainty descend upon you. Thoughts like, "I'm not capable enough," "I'm bound to fail," or "People will judge me," echo in your mind, restraining you from pursuing your dreams. These are examples of limiting beliefs.

A curious blend of creativity and boundless imagination defined my childhood. As far as I can remember, I always had an undeniable passion for creating art. I cherished the tranquil hours spent alone, brushing vibrant hues onto a blank canvas, transforming it into a tapestry of my heart's expressions.

Every stroke was a testament to my creativity and a source of deep pride.

One day, under the scrutinizing gaze of my art teacher, this narrative changed. "This isn't good enough, Luna," she said, looking at one of my paintings with a nonchalant shrug. Her words, meant to be a critique, took on a life of their own. They weaved themselves into the essence of my being, manifesting as a crippling self-doubt that began to overshadow my love for art. I began to question my abilities and my talent. And slowly, the canvases remained blank, the brushes dried, and the colors faded.

This single comment from my art teacher catalyzed a huge personal paradigm shift. My limiting beliefs took root in the fertile soil of this critique and started branching out to other areas of my life. Every aspiration seemed too far-fetched, every dream too grand, every risk too precarious. This paralyzing fear of not being "good enough" followed me like an ominous shadow, making me hold back, and preventing me from pursuing my dreams.

Is this narrative familiar to you? Do you too carry the weight of self-doubt that keeps you from realizing your dreams? We often underestimate the power of limiting beliefs in our lives. They lurk in the recesses of our minds, whispering words of fear and failure, nudging us away from the path of risks and opportunities.

Fast forward to my adulthood, my dream of practicing life coaching emerged. The excitement was palpable, as was the echoing chorus of self-doubt. The old refrain played in my mind, "You're not good enough. You'll fail. People won't trust an inexperienced coach like you."

My limiting beliefs, born from a casual remark in an art class, were now towering around me. The path to my dreams looked like a bewildering maze, every turn leading to a dead end. But with time and much introspection, I realized these walls were not made of stone or concrete; they were self-imposed barriers of my own making, and it was in my power to dismantle them, brick by brick.

You may have experienced similar struggles, let opportunities pass by, and let dreams remain just dreams, all because your self-doubt whispered, "You can't." The pain and regret that come with knowing you've held back from reaching for what you truly desire must also be familiar.

Over time, through consistent effort and the right mindset, I managed to dismantle these barriers. Please believe that you can too; it is why I wrote this book. This journey is about recognizing your limiting beliefs, challenging them, and ultimately breaking free. I'll guide you through it using practical, effective strategies that have transformed my life and those of my clients.

Identifying and overcoming limiting beliefs is like removing the handcuffs that have been restraining your potential. Imagine finally being free to run toward your dreams with a renewed confidence and resilience that nothing can deter. That is the purpose of this book: to release you from the shackles of self-doubt and limiting beliefs and allow your unrealized potential to soar.

Before we can overcome these limiting ideas, we must define them. What holds us back are our preconceived notions of who we are and the world around us. They are usually ingrained during our early years, and over time, become so habitual that we barely notice their presence, let alone challenge them. For instance, if you grew up in an environment where making mistakes was severely punished, you might grow up with the limiting belief that "If I make a mistake, I am a failure." This belief can hold you back from trying new experiences or taking on challenges due to the fear of failure.

Understanding the origins of these limiting beliefs can help in overcoming them. They often stem from our early life experiences, family values, and education and are also significantly influenced by social conditioning—the norms, values, and beliefs that society imposes on us. For instance, societal standards of beauty or success can cultivate limiting beliefs such as, "I'm not beautiful enough" or "I'm not successful unless I have a certain job or amount of wealth."

The path to freedom begins with awareness. By making a conscious effort to identify and understand your limiting beliefs, you start the process of deconstructing them. Remember, every wall is made of individual bricks. By removing each brick—each limiting belief—one at a time, we can bring down the walls that confine us.

In the following pages, we will go into the inner depths of our psyche to explore the consequences of these limiting beliefs on our lives, and most importantly, how we can start to overcome them. Prepare for a journey that will bring you closer to your true self, one of transformation and growth. Hold tight; the road might be challenging, but the rewards are beyond measure. As you turn the pages of this book, remember that each word and each exercise is a step toward your freedom and a life free of limiting beliefs.

Your journey to breaking free begins now.

1A. UNDERSTANDING THE ROOT OF LIMITING BELIEFS

Like a farmer plucking weeds from the soil, you need to recognize these detrimental thoughts before you can start removing them. Limiting beliefs are insidious. They are negative narratives that exist in your subconscious, directing your actions, decisions, and perceptions of yourself and your abilities. They continuously whisper, "You can't do it" or "It's safer not to try," and permeate every area of our lives, inhibiting personal growth and potential.

You might recognize some of these limiting beliefs as they echo in your mind: "I must be perfect to be accepted," "I always mess up," or "Success is meant for others, not for me." These thoughts, which we often accept without question, bind us and restrict our potential to progress.

The Roots of Your Limiting Beliefs

Your limiting beliefs have roots. They are not spontaneous apparitions and are often rooted in your childhood experiences and early learning. Family values and beliefs significantly influence these thoughts. For instance, if your family valued conformity over individuality, you probably grew up believing you needed to blend in to be accepted. If achievement was overemphasized, you probably internalized the belief that your worth is tied to your success, making failure an unacceptable, devastating prospect.

Life experiences also play a substantial role in forming these deep-rooted beliefs. A single negative encounter, such as failing a test, can plant the seed of a limiting belief like "I'm not smart enough." Over time, if such thoughts are not challenged, they can solidify, affecting your confidence in your intellectual abilities and, consequently, your academic or professional pursuits.

Education is a significant contributor to our limiting beliefs too. You might have had a teacher who believed that only certain individuals are creative or that math is a subject only some brains are wired for. Without realizing it, you may have adopted these beliefs as truth, setting up invisible barriers for yourself.

The Impact of Social Conditioning

It's not just your personal experiences and learned values that shape these limiting beliefs. Social conditioning plays a pivotal role in their formation.

Society, often through media, promotes particular narratives and standards. It perpetuates certain stereotypes like "Men don't cry" or establishes superficial standards of beauty, leading to beliefs like "I'm not attractive enough." These societal expectations and norms exert pressure, shaping our perceptions of ourselves and what we deem achievable or acceptable.

Take a moment and reflect on these aspects. What family values were instilled in you growing up? How might your past experiences or education have contributed to any self-doubt or fears you face today? In what way has societal conditioning influenced your self-perception? The answers to these questions might bring forth some of your own limiting beliefs.

It is important to remember that these beliefs are not concrete truths but merely perceptions, shaped by several factors over time. As such, they can be reshaped and replaced with empowering beliefs that promote growth and freedom. In the following chapters, we will explore practical strategies to deconstruct these barriers and replace them with beliefs that serve you and align with your unlocked potential.

The Promise of Personal Transformation

This journey might seem daunting at first but remember that discomfort often accompanies growth. Embrace the pain you feel along the way because it is evidence of how far you've come. I and numerous others have braved this path before, and I promise you that you will not only endure the discomfort but also transform into your best self. Challenging your ingrained, built-in responses and actively changing your attitudes and habits are essential steps toward reshaping your entire identity and overcoming your limiting beliefs. Through each struggle and triumph, you will find yourself moving closer to a life not governed by fear or self-doubt but by self-assurance, resilience, and fulfillment. This is your journey to overcoming your limiting beliefs, and it begins right here, right now.

How Limiting Beliefs Impact Our Lives

Diving deeper, let's further dissect how these limiting beliefs, shaped by the outlined factors, can impact our daily lives. These internal barriers don't exist in a vacuum. They intertwine with your self-perception, actions, and responses to life events and ultimately, shape your reality. For example, if you harbor the belief that "I'm not a people person," it may deter you from seeking or enjoying social inter-actions, which can lead to feelings of loneliness or isolation.

Limiting beliefs can be especially detrimental in the context of personal or career growth. If you're convinced that "I'm not leadership material," you're likely to shy away from opportunities for advance-ment, thereby stagnating your professional progress. This self-limiting narrative keeps you stuck in your comfort zone, preventing you from realizing your full potential.

The Emotional Toll of Limiting Beliefs

Our limiting beliefs also influence our emotions. They can amplify feelings of stress, anxiety, and dissatisfaction as we continuously struggle to meet the unrealistic standards we've set for ourselves. For instance, the belief "I must be perfect to be loved" can lead to constant self-criticism and feelings of inadequacy, affecting our relationships and mental health.

It's crucial to recognize that limiting beliefs aren't always overtly negative. They may seem protective or even reasonable. You might tell yourself that you avoid making speeches because "it's just not your thing." On the surface, this belief may seem innocuous, a simple acceptance of your preferences. But if it's born out of fear of judgment or failure, it's a limiting belief preventing you from developing a skill or achieving personal growth.

Furthermore, our limiting beliefs can have a domino effect. One limiting belief can reinforce others, creating a dense web of self-doubt and fear. For instance, if you believe that "I'm not good enough," it may lead to other limiting beliefs such as "I don't deserve success" or "No one will love me." Over time, these intertwined beliefs can generate a self-fulfilling prophecy. Your actions, driven by these beliefs, will align with them, reinforcing their perceived validity.

Understanding the extent of the impact of such limiting beliefs on our lives is crucial to overcoming them. They not only hinder our personal and professional growth but also impact our emotional well-being and quality of life.

I want you to take a moment and imagine a life free from these constraints. A life where you're not held back by fear or self-doubt, one where you're confident, resilient, and unafraid to pursue your dreams and passions. This life isn't a mere fantasy; you can make it. But to achieve it, you must first confront your limiting beliefs, understand their roots, and gradually learn to replace them with empowering beliefs that promote personal growth and happiness.

Let's step together into a world where you are not confined by your doubts but empowered by your capabilities and potential. However, before we dive in, it is essential to understand the extent of the toll that these limiting beliefs take on our lives.

1B. THE COST OF LIMITING BELIEFS

We all pay a significant price when we allow our limiting beliefs to govern our lives. These deeply entrenched notions we hold about who we are, what we're capable of, and the universe we inhabit can cast a long, constraining shadow over our lives. When you continuously believe that you're "not attractive enough" or "not smart enough," it's like wearing a pair of dark glasses that distort your perception of yourself and the world around you. You start seeing everything through a lens of inadequacy, skewing your self-image to the point where you may fail to recognize your worth, strengths, and capabilities. Just like optical illusions influence and distort your perception, your mind can also perceive things in any way it chooses.

Self-doubt is another hefty price we pay for harboring limiting beliefs. Doubting yourself can be like a chronic, nagging pain that eats away at your confidence, making you second-guess every decision and every action. It breeds fear and hesitation, creating a cycle where you're constantly questioning yourself, which in turn, reinforces your limiting beliefs. This cycle can make you feel trapped in your own mind, breeding feelings of helplessness and stagnation.

Motivation, that vital fuel for achieving our goals and aspirations, also shrinks under the weight of limiting beliefs. If you believe that "success is beyond my reach" or "I'm destined to fail," your drive to strive for better can dwindle. It becomes a self-fulfilling prophecy where the belief that you can't achieve success leads to a lack of effort, which in turn, leads to actual failure, reinforcing the initial limiting belief.

Restrictive Perspective and Unfulfilled Potential

Limiting beliefs restrict our perspective. They act as blinders, narrowing our vision and blocking us from seeing the full range of possibilities and opportunities around us. For instance, the belief that "I'm not creative" can prevent you from exploring and discovering potential talents or passions in the arts or other creative fields. This narrowed perspective can make the world seem smaller, grayer, and less inviting.

The cumulative effect of these influences is a life full of regret and unrealized potential. Every time you allow a limiting belief to dictate your actions, you may miss a chance for growth, learning, success, or happiness. You might pass up a job opportunity because of the belief that you won't "fit in" or avoid expressing your feelings to someone due to the fear of rejection, which stems from the belief that you're "not lovable."

Effects of Limiting Beliefs on Career, Relationships, and Personal Growth

Now, let's discuss how our limiting beliefs can affect specific areas of our lives. In our careers, these beliefs might lead us to settle for less than what we deserve or are capable of. If you believe that you do not possess leadership skills, you might never apply for a managerial role, limiting your career growth. In relationships, the belief that "I'm not worthy of love" can keep you from forming deep, meaningful connections with others. You might push people away, fearing that they'll leave once they "discover" your perceived inadequacies.

Personal growth is perhaps the area most significantly affected by limiting beliefs. Our growth is inherently tied to our willingness to take chances, experience something new, and leave our safe spaces. But if you're shackled by beliefs like "I can't handle failure" or "I'm not adaptable," it becomes almost impossible to embark on this journey of growth.

The relationship between limiting beliefs and negativity is symbiotic. They feed off each other in a destructive cycle. These beliefs often manifest as negative self-talk, your inner critic who is always ready to point out your flaws and remind you of your perceived limitations. This negative self-talk, in turn, reinforces your limiting beliefs, giving them more power over your thoughts, emotions, and actions.

The Heavy Burden of Limiting Beliefs

To further illustrate the consequences of limiting beliefs, let's dive a bit deeper into the context of our everyday lives. Imagine you're walking around with a backpack filled with heavy stones, each one representing a limiting belief and adding to the weight you carry around daily. This burden may eventually become so heavy and cumbersome that you can't even move forward, progress, or stand up straight. This is exactly what limiting beliefs do to us—they weigh us down, restricting our movement and hindering our growth.

Limiting beliefs can cause significant harm to our physical and mental health. For instance, the belief that "I don't have time to take care of myself" can lead to neglecting your health, resulting in stress, fatigue, and other potential health problems. Similarly, if you believe that "seeking help is a sign of weakness," you might ignore early warning signs of mental health issues and fail to seek the help you need.

Dampening the Joys of Life

Even the simple joys of life can be tarnished by these beliefs. For example, the belief that "I should always be productive" can make you feel guilty for taking time out for leisure activities, robbing you of the joy and relaxation they bring.

Furthermore, limiting beliefs can also kill off originality and imagination. If you believe that "I'm not a creative person" or "my ideas are not good enough," you might withhold your thoughts and ideas and refrain from contributing to your full potential in your personal and professional life. This is not just a loss for you but also for those who could benefit from your unique insights and ideas.

Overall, the costs of limiting beliefs taint every aspect of our lives. They cast a dark cloud over our potential for growth, fulfillment, and happiness. However, recognizing these costs is the first step toward liberation. As we journey through this book,

I will provide you with the tools and techniques to unload these heavy stones from your backpack and make your journey through life lighter, freer, and more fulfilling.

1C. PEELING BACK THE LAYERS: STRATEGIES FOR UNCOVERING YOUR LIMITING BELIEFS

Unearthing our limiting beliefs is much like peeling back the layers of an onion. We start on the surface, but as we do the inner work, we encounter more profound, often hidden aspects of ourselves. It's crucial to understand that this process requires honesty and bravery as you're about to embark on a journey of self-discovery. This journey might sometimes be challenging, but it's essential to remember that self-awareness is the first step to overcoming our limiting beliefs. Once we're aware of these subconscious assumptions, we can begin to question and replace them with more positive, growth-promoting beliefs.

Before we jump into specific techniques, it's important to cultivate an attitude of non-judgmental curiosity toward your thoughts and beliefs. Permit yourself to think freely and without criticism.

Remember, these beliefs were formed without your conscious choice, so blaming yourself for having them serves no purpose other than to create an additional limiting belief!

First Technique: The Out-Of-Body Method

As we delve into our exploration of uncovering limiting beliefs, one technique that is particularly illuminating is the "Out-of-Body" method. This approach, which might seem peculiar at first, taps into the power of observation, allowing us to become detached viewers of our own lives.

Much like a director critically analyzing a scene from a film, the Out-of-Body method invites you to adopt a third-person perspective toward yourself. As you step outside your immediate experiences and emotions, you begin to observe your actions and reactions as an outsider would. It's as though you're watching a movie of your life playing out, observing your character with curiosity, compassion, and understanding. This change of perspective can offer striking insights that may otherwise be overlooked in the thick of personal involvement.

The secret to this method is based on observing patterns in your behavior. Let's consider an example.

Suppose you notice that every time you are offered a leadership role at work, you decline and suggest someone else take up the opportunity, even though you're fully qualified for the role. From an outside perspective, you might observe this repeated action and start to question why you continually bypass such opportunities. Is it due to a lack of confidence or fear of failure? Or maybe a belief that you're not deserving of a leadership role? These questions can lead you to unearth the limiting belief that "I'm not competent enough to lead."

This method also requires a keen focus on the situations that cause you distress or lead you to act in ways that contradict your true desires. Such moments of discomfort and resistance are often revealing. For instance, if you find yourself feeling deeply anxious during social gatherings, even though you genuinely enjoy socializing, you might start to question what's at the root of this anxiety. Could it be a fear of judgment? Or perhaps a belief that you're inherently uninteresting? By applying the Out-of-Body method, you could identify the potential limiting belief "People won't find me interesting."

Furthermore, this approach allows you to explore the potential triggers for these beliefs. Using our previous example, you might notice that your anxiety during social gatherings spikes when you're around certain individuals who seem particularly judgmental or when you're expected to talk about yourself. Recognizing these triggers can provide more clues to the limiting beliefs hidden beneath the surface.

Second Technique: The Fill-In-The-Blank Method

The second technique is "The Fill-in-the-Blank" method. This introspective approach thrives on self-interrogation and honesty because it makes use of a simple yet powerful fill-in-the-blank statement: 'I can't achieve/be/have _____ because _____.'

This method is like venturing into the forest of your mind, equipped with a mental flashlight. Each 'blank' in the statement represents an unexplored corner that could be home to a limiting belief. By illuminating these corners, you're likely to unearth beliefs that you were previously unaware of or have been sidestepping.

To illustrate how this method works, let's consider a few examples. Imagine you've always dreamt of starting your own business, but every time the opportunity arises, you find reasons to postpone it.

If you were to complete the statement, it might look something like this: "I can't start my own business because I might fail." This statement reveals a deep-rooted fear of failure which is holding you back from starting your own business.

Another instance could be someone who struggles with maintaining relationships. Their completed sentence might be "I can't maintain relationships because people always end up leaving me." This statement exposes a limiting belief that they are destined to be abandoned, impacting their ability to form and sustain healthy relationships.

Similarly, suppose you've always had a desire to travel the world, but this dream remains unfulfilled. Applying the Fill-in-the-Blank method might result in a statement like, "I can't travel the world because it's not safe," thus revealing a limiting belief related to the perceived dangers of traveling, keeping you from embarking on potentially enriching adventures.

What makes the Fill-In-The-Blank method so effective is its ability to give form to vague fears and uncertainties. By forcing you to articulate the reasons behind your perceived inability to achieve, be, or have something you desire, it reveals the fears you've been hiding.

The Role of Journaling

Journaling serves as an indispensable companion on this journey of uncovering and understanding your limiting beliefs. Imagine your journal as a confidante and silent listener who knows your thoughts and beliefs and helps you navigate the complex terrains of your subconscious. Journaling is a tool that aids memory, fosters self-analysis, and provides a space for contemplative solitude.

As you put pen to paper, chronicling your observations from the Out-of-Body method and the statements crafted using the Fill-In-The-Blank method, you invite reflection and introspection. There is power in manifesting your thoughts on paper—what once seemed nebulous in your mind acquires form and substance, creating a tangible record of your internal journey.

To create a clear map of your limiting beliefs, consider dividing them into categories, like the compartments of a ship. These compartments might include diverse areas of your life, such as career, relationships, and personal growth. The purpose here is to comprehend the territories in your life where your limiting beliefs are most influential and impactful.

However, your expedition does not end there. After cataloging your beliefs, delve deeper into the emotional landscapes they inhabit. Write about the feelings these beliefs stir within you—perhaps they evoke sadness, fear, or even a strange sense of relief. Scale your conviction in these beliefs, rating them from 1 to 10. This practice will enable you to pinpoint the beliefs that resonate most profoundly with you, those that you deem irrefutable truths about yourself and your reality.

From them, focus on the top three. These represent the most formidable walls confining your potential. For each of them, engage in a deeper dialogue with yourself, using your journal as a conduit for the conversation. Ask yourself:

1. Where did this belief come from?
2. How does it affect my actions and emotions?
3. What evidence supports this belief?
4. Is there evidence that contradicts this belief?
5. Would my life be different if I didn't hold this belief?

6. What self-empowering belief can I replace this limiting belief with?

Application of Techniques

By decoding your beliefs through these questions, you challenge their validity and explore the possibility of alternative, more empowering beliefs. This process is a critical step in breaking free from the shackles of your limiting beliefs and creating a mindset that supports your personal growth and success.

Now, having understood the techniques and exercises, you're well-equipped to identify and challenge your limiting beliefs. However, understanding is just the first step. The real magic happens when you apply these learnings consistently. So, I encourage you to begin this journey today. Remember, every step you take, no matter how small, brings you closer to a life free from the confines of your limiting beliefs.

As you continue on this journey, you will likely encounter resistance. Your mind may try to convince you that these beliefs are an integral part of who you are, but remember, you are not your beliefs. They are merely thoughts you've accepted as truth over time. So, when you feel resistance, gently remind yourself that you're on a path of self-discovery and growth and each challenge brings you one step closer to becoming the person you aspire to be.

Now, let's dive into the second part of the exercise. Once you've identified your top three limiting beliefs, it's time to challenge and disprove them. This may seem daunting, especially if these beliefs have been part of your self-perception for a long time. However, remember that these beliefs are not facts but interpretations of past experiences.

Take one belief at a time. Ask yourself, "Is this belief absolutely and universally true?" Remember, we're not looking for examples where the belief might hold; instead, we're searching for a single instance where the belief doesn't apply. For example, if your limiting belief is, "I always fail," ask yourself, "Have I truly failed at everything I've ever attempted?" Most likely, the answer will be no. You'll find instances where you've succeeded, and where you've done well. Hold onto these instances as they're proof that your limiting belief is not an absolute truth.

After challenging your beliefs, the next step is to identify an empowering belief to replace each limiting one. It's not enough to simply disprove your limiting beliefs; you must fill the space they occupy with something new. Without this, you risk falling back into old ways. This empowering belief should be positive, personal, and most importantly, believable. So instead of "I always fail," you could say, "I have the ability to succeed, and every attempt brings me closer to my goals."

However, replacing a deeply ingrained limiting belief with an empowering one is not an overnight process. It requires patience, persistence, and lots of practice. You've been living with these beliefs for a long time, and it will take time to replace them fully.

Each time you notice yourself falling prey to a limiting belief, gently correct yourself with your new empowering belief. Reinforce these new beliefs through affirmations and visualizations and by taking actions that align with them. For instance, if your new belief is, "I have the ability to succeed," then act like someone who is successful: Challenge yourself to take on new tasks, step out of your comfort zone, and embrace opportunities for growth.

Remember, the goal isn't to eliminate all negative thoughts but to foster a mindset where positive, empowering beliefs are the norm rather than the exception. As you practice, you'll find that your thoughts naturally gravitate toward the positive, and over time, these new beliefs will influence your actions and align your reality with your aspirations.

These exercises and techniques are not a one-and-done process but an ongoing journey of self-improvement. It's like strengthening a muscle—the more you exercise it, the stronger it gets. So, the more you practice identifying, challenging, and replacing your limiting beliefs, the better you'll get at fostering a growth mindset.

Through this process, not only can you overcome the limiting beliefs that have held you back, but you'll also develop the tools to tackle any future limiting beliefs that take root. Remember, the power to change your beliefs and therefore, your life, lies within you. By taking the first step on this journey, you're demonstrating the courage and resilience that are the hallmarks of growth. And with every step, you move closer to the person you truly want to become.

1D. INTERACTIVE ELEMENT

In the process of uncovering your limiting beliefs, an interactive tool such as journaling can be of profound value. Journaling allows you to document your thoughts, beliefs, and experiences in a tangible way, facilitating deeper introspection and awareness. More importantly, it allows you to track your progress and witness your growth and transformation as you journey from self-imposed limitations to a life of abundance and fulfillment.

As you progress on this journey, it's essential to engage in the process of self-discovery. The following journal prompts can help with this. They offer specific starting points for exploration and reflection and are designed to help you slow down and engage with your inner world sincerely, so don't answer them hastily.

With these purposes in mind, let's delve into five journal prompts tailored to help you uncover your limiting beliefs.

1. When I think about my biggest dreams and goals, what fears or doubts emerge?

This question urges you to dig deep into the uncertainties that might arise when you contemplate your aspirations. It's important to be honest and transparent in this reflection, as it may reveal beliefs that are hindering your progress.

2. In which areas of my life do I feel stuck?

This query prompts introspection into areas where you might be experiencing stagnation. Is there a particular aspect of your life where you feel you aren't growing or moving forward? The answer could lead you to a limiting belief acting as a roadblock.

3. What beliefs about myself were instilled in me during childhood, and how might they be influencing me today?

This is an opportunity to reflect on early life experiences and how they shaped your perceptions about yourself and the world. You might discover some long-standing beliefs that no longer serve your current goals and values.

4. When I face rejection or failure, what thoughts dominate my mind?

Your response to setbacks can provide profound insights into your limiting beliefs. This prompt encourages you to examine the internal narrative that surfaces during difficult moments.

5. What do I frequently say or think about myself that are negative or self-limiting?

We often express our limiting beliefs through the language we use to describe ourselves and our abilities. This question invites you to recognize patterns in your self-talk that may indicate limiting beliefs.

These prompts serve as an invitation to delve deep into your consciousness, bringing to light the unseen beliefs that may be controlling your life. Be patient with yourself as you navigate this introspective process. Some answers may come quickly, while others might need time to surface. Trust in the process and remember that the journey of self-discovery is not linear but rather a spiral that can sometimes lead you back to old thoughts and feelings. However, with each cycle, you'll gain deeper insights, clarity, and understanding, aiding you in your journey to overcome your limiting beliefs.

1E. KEY TAKEAWAYS

In this first chapter, we discovered how limiting beliefs harm your self-perception, motivation, and outlook on life and frequently impede your progress and success. We also learned how they quietly pervade various aspects of your life, from your career and relationships to your personal development.

Here are our key takeaways:

- Limiting beliefs are closely related to negative self-talk and influence your self-perception and actions.
- The first step toward overcoming these beliefs is to increase self-awareness.
- Techniques like 'Out-of-Body' and 'Fill-in-the-Blank' help uncover ingrained beliefs.
- Journaling is a terrific way to keep track of, categorize, and rate your beliefs.
- Growth requires the process of challenging and replacing limiting beliefs with self-empowering ones.

2

CHANGE YOUR MINDSET,
CHANGE YOUR LIFE

The human mind, with its remarkable power and influence, serves as the architect of our realities. Our thoughts and beliefs act as the blueprint, shaping our actions, attitudes, and ultimately, the world we experience. However, the complexity of this mental landscape is often underappreciated. Shockingly, studies from the National Science Foundation reveal that a staggering 80% of our thoughts are negative, and perhaps more worryingly, 95% are repetitive (Simone, 2017). This implies that we are continuously, though subconsciously, reinforcing negative beliefs about ourselves and our abilities.

These unsettling statistics underscore the pivotal role of our thought processes in our lives. Often, we unknowingly act as our own worst enemies, forti-fying limiting beliefs that constrain our potential and hinder our progress.

The challenge, therefore, lies in finding a way out of this mental labyrinth by recognizing our mind's power to create reality and harnessing this power to foster personal growth and well-being. We must change the narrative in our minds from "I can't" to "I can" and "I will."

However, changing deeply entrenched beliefs is not easy. It's common to encounter obstacles such as fear of change, which involves resistance to new ideas or perspectives; confirmation bias, which is the tendency to interpret information based on our pre-existing beliefs; and lack of self-awareness, which makes it difficult to identify and challenge negative thought patterns and behaviors.

This chapter explores strategies to overcome these obstacles and ultimately, our limiting beliefs. Through this journey, we'll challenge negative self-talk, use powerful tools like visualization, and promote a growth mindset. The goal is to equip you with the knowledge and tools necessary to trans-form your mindset and, consequently, your life.

2A. POSITIVE SELF-TALK

The power of language extends beyond the boundaries of interpersonal communication and shapes our intrapersonal communication, which is the ongoing dialogue in our minds that significantly influences our perceptions and experiences of reality. This inner conversation, often referred to as self-talk, is instrumental in shaping our beliefs and attitudes. Unfortunately, when left unchecked, it can become a breeding ground for negative and limiting beliefs.

By consciously steering this self-talk in a positive direction, we can drastically alter our mental landscape. Positive self-talk is far more than just a cosmetic change of words or forced positivity. It's a fundamental shift in the underlying beliefs that give birth to our thoughts. When you intentionally engage in positive self-talk, you can counterbalance the negative narrative that solidifies your limiting beliefs, replacing it with a narrative of possibility and potential.

Positive self-talk is a cornerstone of a growth mindset—the belief that our abilities and intelligence can be honed and enhanced through consistent effort and perseverance. If you adopt this mindset, you can start viewing challenges not as insurmountable obstacles but as opportunities for growth and development.

Moreover, positive self-talk has several benefits: It fosters a more optimistic outlook, boosts self-confidence, and enhances emotional resilience, thereby improving overall well-being. It also helps manage stress, enhance performance, and maintain a positive mindset, even in the face of adversity.

Switching from negative to positive self-talk requires a conscious effort and the application of several key strategies.

The first strategy involves reality testing, where you assess the accuracy of your negative thoughts by comparing them to facts. For instance, if you find yourself thinking, "I always mess things up," pause and consider the evidence. Have you truly botched every endeavor you've undertaken, or are there instances of success that contradict this belief? More often than not, you'll find that your negative self-talk is based on exaggerated perceptions and not factual evidence. By engaging in reality testing, you can dispel these unfounded negative beliefs and replace them with a more accurate and balanced view of your capabilities.

The second strategy involves searching for alternative explanations or perspectives that challenge your negative assumptions. You must consider other factors that probably contributed to a negative outcome and recognize that it is natural for everyone to make mistakes and experience setbacks when learning. Thus, you can shift your perspective from a self-defeating outlook to one of learning and resilience.

The third strategy is about putting things into perspective. Often, our negative self-talk blows things out of proportion. However, by stepping back and looking at the larger picture, you can gain a more realistic perspective. Ask yourself, "Will this matter in a week, a month, or a year?" Consider the potential consequences of your thoughts and actions. If you find that your self-talk is focusing on insignificant matters or worst-case scenarios that are unlikely to happen, it's time to readjust your perspective to align with reality.

The last strategy involves adopting goal-directed thinking. Instead of ruminating over problems, you must focus on finding solutions. Aim to identify steps that can be taken to improve any situation, rather than dwell on the negative aspects. For instance, instead of thinking, "I'm terrible at this," you might say, "I'm not as skilled at this as I'd like to be yet, but I can improve with practice and effort."

2B. COGNITIVE BEHAVIORAL TECHNIQUES TO CHALLENGE AND REFRAME NEGATIVE THOUGHTS

In the journey toward reshaping our mindsets, cognitive behavioral techniques, particularly cognitive restructuring and behavioral activation, serve as valuable allies. These tools provide practical strategies to identify, challenge, and reframe the negative thoughts that give rise to limiting beliefs.

Cognitive Restructuring

Cognitive restructuring is a key technique that helps us dissect our negative thoughts, examine the evidence supporting them, question their validity, and eventually develop a more balanced perspective. At its core, cognitive restructuring challenges the accuracy of negative thoughts. It prompts us to ask: "Are these negative thoughts true?" If the answer is no, we are encouraged to generate positive counter-thoughts.

Step 1: Enter a State of Quietude

Embarking on the path of cognitive restructuring begins with achieving a state of calm. This initial step is crucial, as it establishes a clear mental environment conducive to introspection and self-aware-ness. You could achieve this tranquility through deep breathing exercises, meditation, or a moment of quietude. The goal is to create a mental space where thoughts can be explored without the inter-ference of immediate emotional reactions.

Step 2: Identifies Your Triggers

Once calm, the next step is to identify what triggers your negative thoughts. This could be a recent event, an upcoming challenge, or even a past interaction. The focus here is not to dwell on the event itself, but rather to discern the circumstances or contexts that prompt negative self-talk. Understanding these trig-gers is the first step toward gaining control over them.

Step 3: Analyze Your Feelings

After you've found your trigger, focus on analyzing your feelings toward the situation. This involves acknowledging and labeling the emotions that are evoked—anxiety, fear, sadness, or frustration. Recognizing these emotional responses is essential, as it provides insight into the impact of the situation and the associated thoughts on your emotional state.

Step 4: Understand Your Thoughts

Next, you must delve deeper into the realm of thoughts, specifically, automatic thoughts or mental responses that arise following the identified situation. They are often reflexive and can go unnoticed unless conscious attention is paid to them. Identifying these automatic thoughts is crucial, as they are often the culprits behind negative self-talk and limiting beliefs.

Step 5: Seek Evidence

Once you've identified your automatic thoughts, it's time to investigate. Your objective is to seek evidence that is factual and can either support or contradict the identified automatic thoughts. You could recall past experiences, verify factual information, or even seek external opinions. The aim is to gather a comprehensive body of evidence that can be used to challenge your negative automatic thoughts.

Step 6: Formulate New Thoughts

With the evidence at hand, the next step is to formulate a more balanced and fair thought. This new perspective is developed by weighing the supporting and contradictory evidence against your automatic thoughts. The goal is not to force a falsely positive thought, but to construct a thought that aligns better with reality. This new thought should be fair, balanced, and less colored by negative bias.

Step 7: Monitor Your Mood

The final phase of cognitive restructuring involves monitoring your current mood. Take a moment to reflect and understand the impact of the restructuring process on your emotional state. Look for any changes in mood or outlook following cognitive restructuring. This not only provides feedback on the effectiveness of the process but also reinforces the ability to influence your mood through cognitive restructuring.

Thus, the process of cognitive restructuring is a journey of self-exploration, analysis, and transformation that provides a strategic pathway to challenge and reframe negative thoughts. It is a powerful tool in the pursuit of a healthier, more positive mindset. The benefits of cognitive restructuring are manifold. It can help reduce anxiety and stress, improve mood, and enhance problem-solving abilities. It can also foster a more positive sense of self and self-esteem as we begin to challenge our negative self-perceptions.

Behavioral Activation

Another powerful cognitive-behavioral technique is behavioral activation. This strategy is based on the premise that our actions influence our thoughts and feelings. It involves engaging in activities that evoke pleasure or a sense of accomplishment, even when feeling unmotivated or negative. These activities serve as direct counterevidence to our limiting beliefs.

Behavioral activation helps disrupt the vicious cycle of negative thoughts that lead to inaction or avoidance behaviors, which in turn, reinforce negative thoughts. By pushing ourselves to engage in activities that bring joy or fulfillment, we generate new evidence that challenges our limiting beliefs and helps reframe our negative thought patterns while boosting confidence and self-efficacy.

Behavioral activation could involve simple activities like taking a walk in nature, reading a book, practicing a hobby, or even completing a small task that has been pending for a while. The key is to select activities that are meaningful and enjoyable. Over time, the sense of accomplishment and positivity derived from these activities can help overshadow negative self-talk, promoting a more positive and proactive mindset.

To enhance the effectiveness of behavioral activation, you must

1. identify activities that are uniquely important to you.
2. ensure the activities are specific and measurable.
3. list activities in order of difficulty.

Incorporating a variety of activities can keep the process engaging, and seeking support from others can add a layer of accountability. Being mindful during these activities, taking things slowly, and rewarding your progress can also significantly bolster the effectiveness of behavioral activation.

Together, cognitive restructuring and behavioral activation provide a comprehensive toolkit to challenge and reframe negative thoughts, offering a powerful means to transform your mindset and the way you perceive yourself.

2C. HARNESSING VISUALIZATION TO OVERCOME LIMITING BELIEFS

The power to change your mindset and overcome limiting beliefs also lies in the unique human ability to visualize. Visualization, or mental imagery, is the process of creating compelling and vivid pictures in your mind. This is not a passive daydream, but rather an active engagement of the mind to imagine achieving a specific goal or overcoming a particular challenge.

The benefits of visualization are numerous and significant. Regular practice can lead to increased self-confidence, heightened motivation, and an enhanced ability to focus on your goals. Furthermore, visualization can help in reducing stress and promoting overall emotional well-being.

Visualization works to overcome limiting beliefs by leveraging the brain's neuroplasticity, an ability to form and reinforce new neural pathways based on experience and learning. When you repeatedly visualize success and positive outcomes, you essentially train your brain to believe that you can achieve those outcomes. You create a new reality in your mind where success is not only possible but also expected, which leads to the creation of new neural pathways that support your newfound, empowering beliefs.

Implementing visualization involves a series of carefully considered steps.

Step 1: What Is Your Goal?

Firstly, you must decide what you want to achieve or what challenge you want to overcome. This forms the basis of your visualization and should be something meaningful and personally significant.

Step 2: What Does It Look Like?

Once you've identified your goal, the next step is to picture it. Create a detailed mental image of the situation where you achieve your goal. Imagine the environment, the people present, the sounds, the smells, and any other relevant sensory details. The more vivid and detailed your mental picture, the more effective your visualization will be.

Step 3: How Will You Reach It?

Next, imagine the journey toward your successful conclusion. Visualize each step you need to take to reach your goal. Feel the actions, the decisions, and the progress in your visualization. This helps to create a sense of realism and attainability in your mind.

Step 4: What Will Achieving It Feel Like?

An important aspect of visualization is replicating the emotion you'll feel on achieving your goal. This helps to cement the belief in your mind that your goal is within reach. It's about experiencing the joy, pride, relief, or any of the other positive emotions associated with your success.

Remember, for visualization to be effective, it must be a regular practice. Set aside time for it each day. Consistency is the key to reinforcing your new beliefs and making them an integral part of your mindset. To maximize the effectiveness of visualization, consider the following tips.

- Choose a quiet environment free from distractions.
- Invoke all your senses to make mental imagery more realistic and engaging.
- Always visualize from a first-person perspective—see the action unfold through your own eyes, not as a detached observer.

- Write down your visualization experiences to keep track of your progress and refine your practice.

2D. POSITIVE AFFIRMATIONS

Positive affirmations are powerful tools to alter one's outlook. They are short, upbeat statements meant to replace negative ways of thinking and shape your attitudes and actions. Consistent use of such affirmations has been shown to alter one's way of thinking over time, leading to an increase in optimism and self-assurance. These positive statements have the power to gradually replace limiting beliefs, broaden one's scope of possibility, and liberate one's full potential.

The negative limiting beliefs that stand in the way of your success can be directly confronted and countered by positive affirmations. By replacing your ingrained negative narratives with positive empowering beliefs, your subconscious can be reprogrammed through the daily practice of positive affirmations. It is the combination of these assertions with the intention or resolve to act that produces the outcomes.

Affirmations are grounded in our knowledge of neuroplasticity. When repeated regularly, positive affirmations have been shown to alter the structure of neural networks in the brain and thus one's way of thinking and perceiving the world around them.

To illustrate the power of positive affirmations, consider the following: "I am capable and strong, and I can handle any challenge that comes my way." Another possible affirmation is, "I deserve to be successful, loved, and happy." Positive self-image and confidence in one's own abilities are the corner-stones of success.

Several rules can be followed to increase the potency of positive affirmations.

- Rule 1: Affirmations must be written in the present tense as if the outcome being sought were already the case. As an alternative to "I will be successful," you could say "I am successful." This makes it easier for your brain to accept the desired state as the current one.
- Rule 2: Affirmations must be genuine and grounded in reality. To make them impactful and believable, they should reflect realistic goals or beliefs that you hold dear.
- Rule 3: Affirmations must be practiced daily to bring out their true potential. Repetition is the key to permanently establishing these ideals in your mind.
- Rule 4: Affirmations must be written in the first person. This makes them more specific to you, which increases their likelihood of having an effect on your subconscious mind.

An illustrative statement would be, "I am resilient and can overcome any obstacle."

- Rule 5: Affirmations must be associated with an emotion or action they are meant to inspire. When you say something like "I am calm and centered," for instance, aim to actually feel peaceful and balanced. Making an emotional connection with the affirmation makes it more powerful in terms of bringing about a shift in perspective.

2E. INTERACTIVE ELEMENT

To bring these concepts to life and embark on your journey of changing your mindset, an interactive element is incorporated into this chapter. This element involves crafting your own set of positive affirmations that align with your goals and the challenges you wish to overcome. The power to transform your mindset lies within you, and taking an active role in creating your affirmations is empowering.

Step 1: Begin this transformative practice by setting aside some quiet time for introspection. Reflect on your personal aspirations, the challenges you face, and the limiting beliefs you wish to overcome. This is a deeply personal process and requires honesty.

Step 2: Once you've identified these, proceed to craft your positive affirmations. These should be concise, positively worded statements that deeply resonate with you. Remember the guidelines discussed earlier for creating effective affirmations: frame them in the present tense, keep them realistic, personalize them, and connect them with feelings or behaviors.

Step 3: Write these affirmations down on a piece of paper, in a journal, or on your digital device. The act of writing solidifies your commitment and helps imprint these affirmations on your mind.

Step 4: Incorporate them into your daily routine. Make a conscious effort to repeat them to yourself throughout the day, especially during moments of calm or introspection. You could do it first thing in the morning, during your breaks in the day, or before you go to bed.

To kickstart your journey, here are a few examples of positive affirmations.

1. "I deserve success and happiness."
2. "I am continually evolving, learning, and growing."
3. "I welcome challenges as they are opportunities for my growth."
4. "I trust my abilities and instincts to guide me."
5. "Each day, I get closer to becoming the best version of myself."

Feel free to use these as they are or modify them to better align with your needs. You can also create entirely new ones that resonate more closely with your journey. The goal of this interactive exercise is to give you hands-on experience in creating and using positive affirmations to help you take active control of your thought processes and initiate a shift toward a more positive empowering mindset. The journey to change your mindset starts with a single step, and crafting your positive affirmations is an excellent place to begin.

2F. KEY TAKEAWAYS

In this chapter, we delved into the power of positive self-talk, explaining how internal dialogue can shape our reality and influence our beliefs. We explored cognitive-behavioral techniques such as cognitive restructuring and behavioral activation, providing practical steps and examples to illustrate how they challenge and reframe negative thoughts. We also unveiled the power of visualization, explaining its principles, benefits, and guidelines for effective practice. Lastly, we presented the power of positive affirmations, encouraging you to craft your own.

This rich tapestry of strategies is designed to empower you to take charge of your thoughts, reshape your beliefs, and set a solid foundation for your personal development. As we conclude this chapter, I hope you feel armed with these tangible strategies and insights and work toward shifting your mindset, transforming your limiting beliefs, and fostering personal growth and well-being. But the journey doesn't end here. In the next chapter, we will delve into the fascinating concept of neuroplasticity and explore how you can harness this intrinsic feature of your brain to further enhance personal growth and navigate toward self-improvement.

3

REWIRING YOUR BRAIN

The mind is everything. What you think, you become.

— BUDDHA

As we begin this chapter, the words of the Buddha, an ancient figure whose teachings have influenced cultures and individuals worldwide, set a fitting tone. It is not uncommon for us to fall into thinking patterns that limit our potential or leave us feeling unworthy. This chapter is dedicated to understanding neuroplasticity, a revolutionary concept that provides a scientific basis to the

Buddha's wisdom and holds the key to liberating ourselves from limiting beliefs.

3A. STRESS, NEGATIVITY, AND THEIR EFFECTS ON THE BRAIN

The mechanics of rewiring our brain hinge upon understanding the effects of pervasive elements such as stress and negativity. Stress, in particular, impacts crucial regions of the brain such as the hippocampus, which manages learning and memory. As Kim et al. (2015) found, extended periods of stress can decrease hippocampal volume, impairing memory and learning abilities. In a working professional's life, chronic stress may cause difficulty in absorbing new information, remembering tasks, or even learning new skills. Additionally, stress pushes the brain to revert to ingrained patterns of behavior, often reinforcing limiting beliefs and negative thought patterns, a survival instinct not particularly useful in today's world.

Exploring the Vicious Cycle of Negativity

The impact of negativity is significant primarily due to the vicious cycle it establishes with stress. The brain's propensity toward negativity biases can lead to stress, further fueling negativity and establishing a self-feeding loop (Baumeister et al., 2001). For instance, even a little negative feedback at work may cloud our perception, causing us to overlook the numerous positive feedback we receive. This can result in stress, which then leads us to anticipate more negative experiences, hence forming a cycle. Consequently, breaking this cycle through conscious effort and positivity is key in using neuroplasticity to reshape our minds.

The Connection Between Stress, Negativity, and Emotional Regulation

We must understand the impact of stress and negativity on our brain's prefrontal regions, which are responsible for functions like decision-making and emotional regulation. Stress and negativity can disrupt connectivity between the dorsal and ventral prefrontal regions, affecting our ability to regulate emotions effectively (Morawetz et al., 2016). For example, under the influence of prolonged stress, we might react more impulsively or struggle to manage our emotions when faced with challenges.

Leveraging Neuroplasticity to Overcome Stress and Negativity

Comprehending the influence of stress and negativity is the first step to leveraging neuroplasticity, as it helps us identify and challenge our detrimental patterns. Our neural networks are influenced by our experiences and mental states. Therefore, constant stress and negativity can reinforce pathways associated with anxiety, fear, and limiting beliefs, thus making it increasingly challenging to break away from these destructive thought patterns (Davidson & McEwen, 2012).

Strategies to Combat Stress and Negativity

Armed with knowledge about the effects of stress and negativity, we can develop strategies to combat destructive thought patterns. Techniques to manage stress effectively, like mindfulness and cognitive-behavioral strategies, can help us reframe our negative thoughts into more constructive ones. To reduce stress levels, consider practicing mindfulness and focusing on the present to minimize rumination over past negative experiences or worries about the future. Furthermore, consciously choosing positivity can rebalance our brain's negativity bias, fostering a balanced perspective that supports our journey toward overcoming limiting beliefs.

Understanding the effects of stress and negativity provides us with the necessary knowledge to face these challenges head-on. As such, we can start to recognize the patterns that stress and negativity perpetuate in our lives and prepare to break free from them.

3B. UNRAVELING THE CONCEPT OF NEUROPLASTICITY

Neuroplasticity, in essence, is the brain's capacity to rewire itself. It refers to the physical changes that occur in the brain in response to learning, experience, or injury. In a practical sense, neuroplasticity implies that we possess the ability to reframe our brain's wiring, fostering fresh patterns of thinking, feeling, and behaving. This ability is our most potent weapon against the restrictive confines of limiting beliefs.

Research has indicated that our actions, thoughts, and emotions can physically alter the brain's structure and function (Dayan & Cohen, 2011). This means that positive thoughts and behaviors, such as practicing mindfulness, can strengthen neural networks associated with happiness, resilience, and self-confidence, offering us a profound way to transform our lives from the inside out.

Neuroplasticity also offers a fascinating perspective on our potential to change. It puts forth the empowering message that we are not doomed to repeat patterns of behavior that limit our growth. This idea directly contradicts the outdated notion that our character traits and behaviors cannot change beyond a certain age, further reinforcing the truth that change is possible at any stage of life (Dayan & Cohen, 2011).

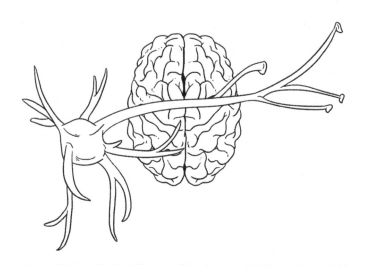

Practical Strategies to Leverage Neuroplasticity

Harnessing the power of neuroplasticity requires mindful and consistent efforts. These efforts comprise habits that promote mental well-being, such as mindful meditation, physical exercise, and positivity.

- **Mindful meditation** is a powerful tool that promotes neuroplasticity. It encourages us to focus on the present, which significantly reduces stress and anxiety levels, the common culprits behind limiting beliefs. Practicing mindfulness engages different areas of our brains, fostering new neural pathways.
- **Physical exercise** supports neuroplasticity by enhancing the overall health of our brains. Regular physical activity can create new neural connections and lead to improved mental toughness and resilience, which are crucial for overcoming limiting beliefs.
- **Positivity** is essential to create the perfect environment for neuroplasticity optimization. Our brains tend to pay more attention to negative experiences, so

deliberately focusing on positive experiences can counteract this bias and rewire our brains to amplify positive thoughts and emotions.

Neuroplasticity plays an essential role in fortifying the neural connections we frequently employ while diminishing the rarely used ones.

The Integral Role of Environment and Lifestyle in Neuroplasticity: Designing a Neurologically Nurturing Atmosphere

The settings in which we find ourselves and the lifestyle choices we make have a significant impact on our brains' abilities to adapt and change in response to experiences. The environment and the way of life we adhere to are two of the most potent influencers in this equation.

To put it simply, our brains flourish when they are exposed to environments that abound with novelty and mental stimulation. These might include interactive experiences, creative pursuits, educational opportunities, and even exploring new physical landscapes. Each of these provides a rich tapestry of sensory and cognitive stimuli that the brain can engage with, encouraging the formation of new neural connections, and thus enhancing neuroplasticity. Additionally, they also serve to boost cognitive function and promote clarity of thought, creativity, and problem-solving capabilities.

That said, adequate rest and sleep are equally crucial for brain health. As you sleep, your body and mind heal and rejuvenate. The brain, especially, consolidates memories, processes the day's experiences, and detoxifies harmful waste products in this time. Thus, lack of adequate sleep can severely impair neuroplasticity and cognitive performance, further solidifying the importance of maintaining good sleep hygiene and ensuring sufficient rest to support the brain's adaptive processes.

Awareness: The Prelude to Personal Transformation

Every journey starts with a single step, and in the quest for cognitive change, the first step is awareness. Awareness involves introspecting and identifying limiting beliefs and negative thought patterns that, while often subtle, exert considerable influence over your life.

This journey of self-discovery is far from straightforward. It requires a strong commitment to self-awareness and the courage to confront the unknown aspects of yourself. You must peel back layers of learned behaviors and habitual thinking patterns to reveal the underlying structures that shape your perceptions of yourself and the world around you.

Reframing: Charting a New Course for Mental Narratives

Once awareness is established, the next step is reframing. Here, we intentionally replace our limiting beliefs and negative thought patterns with those that promote growth and self-efficacy. The goal isn't merely to adopt a positive mindset but rather to foster realistic and enabling thoughts that align with our core values and life goals.

Now comes the hard part of making changes. You must challenge long-held beliefs, question ingrained assumptions, and actively choose thoughts that better serve your aspirations. It's all about rewriting the narrative of your inner world and crafting a mental landscape that encourages personal growth, resilience, and fulfillment.

Reinforcement: Solidifying New Pathways for Empowered Thinking

The final phase in leveraging neuroplasticity is rein-forcement. This involves actively engaging with the new, empowering narratives and integrating them into your daily thoughts and actions until they become second nature. Remember, your brain strengthens new connections and weakens old ones through repetition, so you must be disciplined and steadfast.

Unleashing the Power of Neuroplasticity: Translating Theory Into Practice

Through the consistent application of these steps, we can tap into the transformative potential of neuroplasticity. When we deliberately choose healthier, more beneficial thought patterns and reinforce them through repetition, we make them the standard framework of our cognitive processes.

As such, we turn theory into practice, utilizing the inherent flexibility of our brains to enhance our quality of life. Neuroplasticity has the remarkable power to change our brains, and thus ourselves, for the better. Through awareness, reframing, and reinforcement, we can break free from limiting beliefs and foster a mindset that supports growth, empowerment, and personal fulfillment.

3C. MINDFULNESS AND ITS TRANSFORMATIVE POWER

Mindfulness has the potential to trigger a substantial increase in regional brain gray matter density. This change is predominantly noticeable in structures integral to learning, memory processes, emotional regulation, self-referential processing, and perspective-taking. In essence, regular mindfulness practice can effectively reshape your brain, enhancing its efficiency in processing information and managing emotions. In a world that frequently feels chaotic and overwhelming, such changes can bring about profound benefits like improved emotional control, heightened focus, and a greater sense of well-being.

Mindfulness: Fostering Emotional Regulation

At its core, mindfulness introduces a sense of objectivity toward our thoughts and emotions. Instead of being engulfed in a whirlwind of emotional reactions, we are encouraged to perceive our thoughts and feelings as transient events. Such a change in perspective empowers us to respond to experiences rather than to impulsively react to them. This self-regulation, driven by mindfulness, could be attributed to changes in brain networks related to self-control (Tang et al., 2015).

Integrating Mindfulness Techniques in Daily Life

Here are a few examples of mindfulness techniques you can practice every day to enhance neuroplasticity and cultivate transformation:

Mindful Breathing

This practice is fundamental to mindfulness techniques. Its main objective is to guide your attention toward the natural rhythm of your breath, devoid of any attempts to control or change it. Feeling your breath as it enters and leaves your body helps to put a healthy distance between you and your worries, both present and future. Research, including a study from Belgium's University of Leuven, indicates that mindful breathing can alleviate stress, amplify attention, and foster emotional well-being.

You can practice several types of mindful breathing techniques to cultivate mindfulness. Here are a few examples:

- Pranayama: This yoga exercise involves controlling your breath to increase awareness and vitality. There are several types of pranayama exercises, including Kapalabhati—rapid, forceful breathing; Bhastrika, bellows breath; and Anulom Vilom alternate nostril breathing.

- Alternate Nostril Breathing: Breathe in and out through alternate nostrils using your fingers to block one nostril as you inhale and the other as you exhale. This practice balances the body and mind and reduces stress and anxiety.
- Deep Breathing: Take slow, deep breaths and focus on clearing your mind of distractions. Deep breathing will tame your fight-or-flight response and help you calm down.
- 4-7-8 Breathing: Inhale while you count to four, then hold your breath for a count of seven, and finally, exhale while you count to eight. This can help to slow down breathing and calm the mind and body.
- Counted Breathing: Count each breath to a specific number, such as four or six. The goal is to focus on counting and the sensation of the breath, which helps calm the mind and reduce stress.
- Equal Breathing: Inhale and exhale for the same amount of time, like four counts in and

four counts out. The goal is to balance breathing, thus creating a sense of calm and relaxation.

- Diaphragmatic Breathing: Focus on breathing deeply into the diaphragm rather than the chest. This can help to slow down breathing and reduce stress and anxiety.
- Progressive Relaxation: Tense and release your muscle groups while focusing on your breath. As you cycle through the muscle groups, this practice releases your physical tension and prepares you for relaxation.

Meditation

Meditation, particularly mindfulness-based meditation, is an exercise that regulates attention. Here, you focus on a single object, such as your breath, a specific word or phrase (a mantra), or even an image.

When your mind begins to wander, this practice will gently guide it back to the object of your focus, thus honing mental discipline, calmness, and overall focus. Regular meditation, according to Hölzel et al. (2011), can lead to structural brain changes, such as increased gray matter density in the hippocampus.

Body Scan

This technique involves focusing systematically on various body parts, from your toes to the top of your head. You're guided to observe any sensations, tension, or discomfort in your body without judgment as you mentally scan. This technique fosters relaxation, well-being, and heightened bodily awareness. Spinelli et al. (2019) found that performing a body scan can alleviate stress, improve well-being, and enhance quality of life.

Mindful Movement

Activities like Yoga and Tai Chi are examples of mindful movement that fuse physical movement with mindfulness. Each movement is performed with full attention and focus on the body's sensations. This practice not only bolsters physical health but also promotes engagement with the now. According to Watts et al. (2018), mindful movement exercises can diminish anxiety, depression, and stress while enhancing psychological well-being.

Mindful Eating

Mindful eating involves concentrating fully on the act of eating, savoring each bite, and being conscious of the tastes, textures, and aromas of your food. It also encompasses recognizing your body's hunger and fullness cues, thus fostering a healthier relationship with food. Research, including a study by Grider et al. (2020), reveals that mindful eating can help reduce binge and emotional eating.

Practicing mindfulness on a regular basis improves cognition, attention, and emotional regulation. As the brain adapts to these practices, it brings about a shift in perspective, replacing old, limiting beliefs with new, empowering ones.

Each mindfulness technique, from mindful breathing to mindful eating, works in harmony to reshape neural pathways, train your brain, manage stress, regulate emotions, and challenge limiting beliefs. They are transformative tools, fostering self-awareness and emotional self-regulation that can help break free from the constraints of limiting beliefs and unlock your hidden abilities.

3D. KEY TAKEAWAYS

In this chapter, we've talked about the importance of neuroplasticity, our brain's incredible ability to change and adapt, and its critical role in personal growth. Understanding the formation and reinforcement of neural pathways provides insight into the challenges and opportunities associated with changing limiting beliefs.

Mindfulness practices like mindful breathing, meditation, body scan, mindful movement, and mindful eating have been studied as powerful tools for changing our brain's wiring and promoting healthier thoughts and behaviors. Each of these practices improves self-awareness, emotional regulation, and neuroplasticity, thus assisting in the replacement of limiting beliefs with empowering ones.

4

QUIETING THE MIND

I swear to you that to think too much is a disease, a real, actual disease.

— FYODOR DOSTOYEVSKY

4A. THE PARALYSIS OF OVERTHINKING

Life, in its beautifully complex nature, often presents us with an intricate dance of thoughts. It's a common experience to find ourselves lost in a whirl of contemplations about our past, present, and future. While pondering about life can be insightful, there's a point where it becomes excessive and leads to overthinking.

Overthinking, characterized by persistent worrying and second-guessing decisions, often results in 'analysis paralysis' where individuals find it challenging to make decisions due to excessive contemplation. It can present various symptoms:

- Mental exhaustion from continuous ruminating thoughts.
- All-or-nothing thinking that leads to stress and missed opportunities.
- Catastrophizing or expecting worst-case scenarios.
- Overgeneralizing past negative experiences when analyzing future events.

Overthinking can be a natural reaction to stress or uncertainty, but it can also indicate anxiety, depression, or other mental health issues. It can result in negative thought patterns, increased tension and worry, difficulties making decisions, and decreased problem-solving ability.

4B. THE ROOT CAUSES OF OVERTHINKING

Navigating our minds' vast landscapes often reveals paths that lead to overthinking, a mental phenomenon that binds and bewilders many. Identifying its root causes is akin to unraveling a complex puzzle, which on completion will offer insight into why the mind sometimes spirals into ceaseless contemplation. That said, the reasons for overthinking are multifaceted and interwoven, creating a tapestry of mental challenges. Here are some root causes that you may identify with.

- Not Being Solution-Oriented: This mindset, lost in problems rather than potential solutions, serves as fertile ground for overthinking, breeding a cycle of stagnation and worry. When you're not focused on finding a solution to a problem, your mind can keep cycling through the same thoughts without making any progress.

- Experiencing Repetitive Thoughts: Like echoes in a canyon, repetitive thoughts bounce and reverberate within the mind, creating a relentless loop that traps you in a state of mental restlessness. This is especially true if the ideas are negative or cause worry.

- Inability to Quiet Your Mind: A mind that refuses to quiet becomes a persistent noise, drowning out clarity and focus and turning the symphony of thoughts into cacophony. One reason your brain may be unable to shut off is due to an imbalance in the neurotransmitters that regulate mood and cognitive function. Additionally, chronic stress and anxiety can lead to an overactive amygdala, which can make it difficult to turn off negative thoughts and feelings.

- Struggling to Decide: When every choice becomes a battle, the struggle to decide amplifies doubt and insecurity, feeding the beast of overthinking. There might be many reasons why you struggle with decision-making—fear of making the wrong decision, being indecisive, or external pressures and expectations.

- Second-Guessing Decisions: The shadow of doubt that follows decisions can turn confidence into uncertainty, leading to a never-ending cycle of questioning and reevaluation.

Understanding these root causes of overthinking is a vital step in the journey to mental clarity, and it helps you untangle your web of thoughts and steer your mind toward tranquility and purpose.

4C. THE MANY FACES OF OVERTHINKING

The signs and symptoms of overthinking are as diverse as the individuals who experience them. Some people find themselves wrestling with the same thoughts or worries for hours on end. Others constantly second-guess their decisions, never feeling confident or convinced with the choices they make. An insidious kind of exhaustion comes with overthinking that can feel like your brain won't switch off, even when you desperately want it to.

More concerningly, overthinking can also lead to all-or-nothing thinking, catastrophizing, overgeneralizing, or ruminating on the past.

All or Nothing

All-or-nothing thinking traps us in a world of absolutes where things are either perfect or a disaster. Such thinking is often linked to perfectionism and can lead to stress, anxiety, and missed opportunities. For example, you may think that if you don't get top scores on a test, you're a failure or if you can't play piano like Beethoven, you shouldn't play at all. Black or white thinking like this hinders personal growth and is toxic to the mind.

Catastrophizing

Here, we exaggerate problems and prepare for the worst. It's like having an annoying stone in your shoe but thinking you're going to lose your foot. Such thinking is often linked to anxiety disorders and can interfere with problem-solving and decision-making skills (American Psychological Association, 2021). For example, if you have a slight quarrel with a buddy, you may think that your friendship has been irreversibly harmed. Overthinking like this can lead to feelings of despair and hopelessness, making it impossible to move on.

Overgeneralizing

When we apply one negative experience to all future ones, we overgeneralize. We think that if we've failed once, we'll fail every time. This can limit our willingness to take risks and undermine our self-confidence. For example, if you've taken a driver's test once and failed or if you've caused a small accident while learning, you'll keep going back to that experience and feel like driving is not meant for you and that you should give it up.

Ruminating

Ruminating on the past can tie us to our old mistakes and regrets, preventing us from enjoying the present and securing a positive future. For example, if you have a negative job interview experience, you may begin to assume that you will never be able to get a decent job and that you are unqualified for any position you may desire. This can make you feel defeated and hinder your motivation.

Research shows that overthinkers tend to have more stress, experience higher levels of anxiety and depression, and struggle with sleep problems (Wilding, 2021). It's a habit that not only causes emotional distress but also has severe implications for health.

4D. THE ROAD TO QUIETING YOUR MIND

Let's unpack this treasure trove of tips and strategies that curb overthinking. Overthinking is not a life-long contract you're stuck with. It's just a habit, and habits can be changed. There's a whole toolbox of techniques and strategies to help you on your journey.

Set Up Worry Periods

One powerful strategy is setting up a worry period (Healthline, 2021). Sounds odd, doesn't it? But it's like scheduling an appointment with your worries. During this specific time each day, you allow yourself to worry, to let those thoughts run wild. However, outside of this period, you train your mind to stay clear of these intrusive thoughts. The trick here is compartmentalizing your worries, giving them a specific time and space, and not letting them invade the rest of your day.

Challenge Negative Thoughts

Another technique involves challenging those negative thoughts and questioning the "what ifs" that often fuel overthinking (Cuncic, 2020). You're not denying your worries but rather confronting them and asking, "Is this worry rational? How likely is it to happen?" This technique encourages a more balanced perspective, helping to diminish the impact of overthinking on your emotions and behaviors.

Distract Yourself

Distracting yourself with hobbies or physical activities is also a valuable strategy (Healthline, 2021). Imagine your brain as a computer with multiple tabs open. A hobby can be a new, exciting tab that diverts attention from the worry tab. Hobbies help us stay in the moment, and by engaging our brains in a different, enjoyable way, they leave little room for rumination. Exercise provides dual benefits. Besides the distraction, it also releases endorphins, our body's natural mood elevators, which can help counteract the stress and anxiety associated with over-thinking.

Practice Mindfulness

Mindfulness practices, such as meditation, are also beneficial (Cleveland Clinic, 2021). They help you become more aware of your thoughts and emotions and observe them without getting entangled in them. It's like watching a movie without getting absorbed in the story. This awareness can reduce the power of overthinking, giving you rather than your thoughts control.

Stay in the Now

Grounding yourself in the present and fully immersing yourself in whatever you're doing right now is another useful tool. It's about being here and now without thinking about what has happened or what will happen. Additionally, practicing self-compassion, forgiveness, and gratitude can shift your perspective, reducing the impact of negative self-talk and enhancing your overall well-being.

4E. JOURNAL YOUR WAY THROUGH

Now, we'll talk about some self-compassion journal prompts. These are guided questions or statements that help you to write reflectively about your thoughts and feelings. For instance, a prompt might be, "Write about a time you felt misunderstood. How can you show kindness to yourself during such moments?" These prompts guide you toward understanding and accepting your feelings, offering you a gentle way to explore and navigate your emotional landscape. By penning your thoughts and emotions, you not only gain a deeper understanding of yourself, but you also create a safe space to process your experiences, which can be an effective tool in overcoming overthinking.

So, while the journey might seem challenging, remember that you've got an arsenal of strategies and techniques to support you. Overthinking might be a habit, but it doesn't define you, and most importantly, it's a habit that can be broken.

Start by using some of these phrases to be kinder to yourself. Think about them and write about your impressions and how each phrase makes you feel.

1. It's okay that I feel a certain way.
2. This experience will help me grow.
3. It's okay that a situation is hard because I will find my way through it.
4. I'll look at this situation from different views before I react.
5. I'm not my thoughts.

Once you spend some time with these phrases and positive affirmations and write your reactions, try some of these journal prompts to truly explore the ideas.

1. What can you take out of your routine that will make your days happier? Will removing this item give you time for self-care?
2. What is one expectation that makes you feel pressured in life?
3. What stress are you currently dealing with? What advice would you give a friend who was facing the same issue? Give that advice to yourself with kindness.
4. What area of life feels most chaotic to you and why? Are there ways you can become more organized in this realm?

5. What is something currently disappointing you in your life? Do you have the power to change it? Write down three ways you could turn your disappointment into a point of success and productivity.

After answering these questions, reflect on how your mindset has changed. Do you feel like you're more positive overall? Do you accept others as they are? Do you give yourself more grace? The overall goal of this interactive exercise should be to experience self-compassion. This quality, in turn, will help you feel kinder toward everyone in the world around you and help you develop a positive outlook in life.

4F. KEY TAKEAWAYS

In Chapter 4, we learned how to quiet our minds and delved into the complexities of overthinking, uncovering its detrimental effects and the means to escape its grasp. Key insights include:

- The Paralysis of Overthinking: Marked by exhaustive contemplation and negative foresight, this can lead to stress, missed chances, and unrealistic negative expectations.

- The Many Faces of Overthinking: It presents in various forms with restrictive patterns like black-or-white thinking, catastrophic predictions, and overgeneralization, each stifling personal growth.

- Causes of Overthinking: The root of overthinking often lies in a lack of solution-oriented thinking, repetitive and unceasing thoughts, a mind that won't quiet, struggles in decision-making, and a tendency to second-guess decisions. These factors intertwine to create a mental whirlpool that keeps individuals stuck in indecision and doubt.

- The Road to Quieting the Mind: Escaping overthinking is achievable through targeted strategies such as setting up worry periods, challenging negativity, engaging in distractions and mindfulness, grounding yourself in the present, and practicing self-compassion and reflective journaling.

Light the Path for Others

"There is one grand lie – that we are limited. The only limits we have are the limits we believe."

— WAYNE DYER

Once I started breaking free from my own limiting beliefs, I began to realize just how common my experience was. I was lucky in that I could trace the roots of my self-doubt back to that art class, but I've talked to so many people who can't pinpoint a catalyst that clearly – and so many others for whom there was no single event, but a cascade of moments that fed into their belief that they weren't good enough.

As soon as we recognize that the beliefs we hold about ourselves are limiting us, we begin to change our trajectory. I'm not saying it's easy, but realizing that you're the one standing in your own way is powerful, and it drives you to address the problem.

That's why you're here reading this book. It's also why I wrote it, and it's why so many other people are looking for the guidance it provides.

While making the decision to conquer those limiting beliefs is powerful in itself, actually rising above them, as I'm sure you know, is much more challenging, and many people don't have a clue where to start. I wrote this book to help them – and now that you're already well into your journey, you're in a great position to help me reach them.

All I need from you is a few minutes of your time and a few quick sentences.

By leaving a review of this book on Amazon, you'll show other people who are ready to move past those limiting beliefs and discover their true potential exactly where they can find the guidance they're looking for.

Simply by letting other readers know how this book has helped you and what they'll find inside, you'll provide the signpost that will show them that the help they're looking for exists.

Thank you so much for your support. You'd be amazed by how many people struggle with this issue.

Scan the QR code to leave a review!

5

UNLEASH YOUR INNER WARRIOR

To uncover your true potential you must first find your own limits and then you have to have the courage to blow past them.

— PICABO STREET

Mental toughness is more important than you may believe. Think of the last few years, with the pandemic, social upheaval, economic problems, and other things you may never have expected to face. Making it through those obstacles requires resilience and grit. If you feel like you're struggling and aren't capable of these feats, never fear—you can empower your inner warrior.

5A. UNDERSTANDING MENTAL TOUGHNESS

The quest for personal growth and dismantling limiting beliefs calls for a guiding star: mental toughness. This intricate trait, often misconstrued as mere resilience, is a potent blend of several psychological skills. It empowers us to tackle high-stakes demands, navigate adversity, and consistently deliver peak performance (Jones et al., 2007).

At the heart of mental toughness lie several core elements:

- Emotional Regulation: Allows you to maintain emotional balance in stressful situations.
- Optimism: Helps you maintain a positive outlook amidst setbacks.
- Self-Belief: Fuels your confidence and conviction in your abilities.

Together, these traits forge the resilient framework of mental toughness, preparing you to meet challenges head-on.

Embracing your inner warrior requires you to draw on your inner reserves of power and perseverance by developing self-assurance, assertiveness, and a resolve to overcome difficulties and achieve personal objectives. Moreover, it requires you to accept vulnerability, confront fears, and learn from setbacks.

The Transformative Power of Mental Toughness

Why does mental toughness play a pivotal role in breaking free from limiting beliefs? The potency of this trait lies in its transformative effects on your self-perception and approach to adversity and life in general.

Mental toughness acts as a catalyst for sustaining high-level performance, even amidst stress and pressure (Gucciardi et al., 2012). It helps you navigate life's inevitable obstacles while fostering a robust belief in yourself, propelling you toward your goals.

As you cultivate this trait, you dismantle fear, self-doubt, and limiting beliefs, paving the way for bravery, conviction, and an indomitable spirit.

Research affirms the many benefits of mental toughness (Crust & Clough, 2005):

- Enhanced stress management
- Improved focus
- Sustained high performance under pressure

These elements are vital in eradicating limiting beliefs, thus underscoring the indispensable role of mental toughness in personal growth.

Mental Toughness in Action

As we journey toward cultivating mental toughness, examining real-life case studies can offer valuable insights. The experiences of those who have walked this path illuminate the transformative power of mental toughness in surmounting self-imposed limitations.

Mental toughness goes beyond common misconceptions of being a mere synonym for resilience or grit. It is, in fact, a sophisticated weave of psychological skills and attributes. The narrative of top-tier athletes or corporate leaders who thrive under pressure illustrates how this trait isn't confined to physical capabilities or strategic prowess alone, but heavily leans on mental toughness.

Mental Toughness: Not Just for the Elite

Contrary to the belief that mental toughness is reserved for high achievers, it is an adaptable trait accessible to everyone (Gucciardi et al., 2012). Regardless of your past or present circumstances, mental toughness can be intentionally honed and strengthened, empowering you to navigate stress and adversity effectively.

Mental toughness affects how you handle adversity and perceive yourself and shapes your life's course. This mental fortitude enables you to operate under pressure, grapple with challenges, and foster an unshakeable belief in your capabilities. Your past experiences or current circumstances don't define your potential to cultivate mental toughness; it's a skill that can be consciously developed and strengthened.

Now, let's dive deeper into why mental toughness is pivotal for overcoming limiting beliefs. In essence, mental toughness primes you for personal growth, freeing you from the constraints of limiting beliefs. It equips you with a resilient mindset, allowing you to approach life with courage and conviction, transitioning you from a reactionary being to a proactive architect of your life.

On unraveling the constituents of mental toughness, we encounter resilience, optimism, emotional control, and self-belief as key components.

Resilience allows you to recover from setbacks, viewing failures as growth opportunities instead of roadblocks. Optimism helps maintain a positive outlook, treating challenges as temporary hurdles. Emotional control lets you manage your emotional responses effectively, retaining composure under pressure. Lastly, self-belief, the unwavering conviction in your abilities, propels you through self-doubt and fear, leading you toward your desired outcomes.

Mental toughness is a culmination of these and other components, forming a psychological armor safeguarding us from the detrimental impacts of stress, adversity, and failure.

The Four Cs of Mental Toughness

Let's dive into the crux of mental toughness, which is broadly classified into four main components: control, commitment, challenge, and confidence. Each of these aspects is instrumental in your journey to transcend limiting beliefs.

Control

Control refers to the ability to regulate your thoughts, feelings, and circumstances effectively. For example, an executive managing a crucial project under tight deadlines exhibits control when they balance the team's stress levels while steering the project in the right direction.

Practical Tip: Incorporate practices like mindfulness, which enhances emotional regulation and self-control.

Commitment

Commitment, the next component, reflects your determination to stick to your goals, notwithstanding the hurdles that come your way. Think of an athlete who, despite an injury, stays committed to their recovery and returns to the sport.

Practical Tip: Foster commitment using the SMART (Specific, Measurable, Achievable, Relevant, Time-bound) goal-setting technique that promotes clarity and dedication.

Challenge

Challenge is all about how you perceive difficulties. Those with a high level of mental toughness welcome challenges, using them as stepping stones toward their goals. A budding entrepreneur, for instance, might view the launch of a competitive product as a challenge to improve their own.

Practical Tip: To enhance this trait, adopt a growth mindset that sees challenges as opportunities.

Confidence

Lastly, your unwavering faith in your own abilities is the bedrock on which confidence rests. Consider the self-assuredness of a seasoned musician about to step onto a stage in front of thousands of fans.

Practical Tip: Bolster confidence through self-affirmation exercises and by reframing your self-perception positively.

The Role of Emotional Intelligence in Mental Toughness

Emotional intelligence illuminates the crucial interplay between emotional acuity and mental toughness. This connection encompasses the perception, comprehension, management, and application of emotions with emotional intelligence serving as an engine propelling mental toughness.

Self-Awareness: The First Step

Self-awareness, or the conscious recognition and understanding of one's emotions, is a cornerstone of emotional intelligence. This critical element helps you understand how your feelings shape your thoughts, decisions, and actions. Heightened self-awareness keeps emotions from driving your decisions astray, allowing you to identify them, comprehend their origins, and weigh their impact before choosing your next step.

Consider a high-stakes poker player, for example. With self-awareness, they recognize their nervousness, understand its roots, and can channel this energy into maintaining a keen focus, turning what could be a hindrance into an advantage.

Emotional Regulation: The Steering Wheel

Emotional regulation refers to our ability to manage emotions according to our goals and the current situation. This skill closely ties into the control aspect of mental toughness. For instance, an entrepreneur weathering the collapse of a venture may regulate emotions to manage disappointment constructively, maintain focus, and find the resilience to start over, embodying mental toughness.

Laborde et al.'s (2016) research confirms the connection between emotional intelligence and mental toughness. Higher emotional intelligence equates to increased mental toughness, thanks to one's ability to understand, manage, and use one's emotions effectively and foster resilience in the face of adversity.

Empathy: Connecting With Others

Understanding empathy, a core component of emotional intelligence, proves beneficial for mental toughness. Empathy not only helps you comprehend others' emotions but also bolsters interpersonal relationships, establishing a support network that fosters emotional resilience in tough times. A team leader who practices empathy, for instance, can better grasp the emotional states of team members, fostering a supportive and cohesive work environment, thus increasing the team's resilience.

Leveraging Emotions to Facilitate Thought

Emotional intelligence provides the skill to leverage emotions to facilitate thought, which is essential for mental toughness. Emotions serve dual roles—they are responses to events and drivers of cognitive processes (Damasio, 1994). Harnessing emotions to guide your thinking integrates emotional responses into cognitive processes, improving your ability to navigate challenges and make sound decisions.

For example, an attorney engaged in a high-pressure court case may leverage their anxiety to prepare more comprehensively, transforming worry into proactive action.

To cultivate emotional intelligence, you must be aware of your emotional state and view it as valuable insight. Treating emotions as informative data better equips you to steer your decisions and actions, instead of being swayed by emotional responses.

Resilience: Turning Adversity Into Advantage

Resilience is the cornerstone of mental toughness. It is the art of adapting positively to adversity, trauma, threats, or significant stress. The goal isn't to avoid stress but rather to learn how to thrive with it.

To foster resilience, developing a positive outlook is crucial. Positive emotions counterbalance the effects of stress and foster quicker recovery (Fredrickson, 2001). You can practice positivity by

- actively seeking out joyful elements in your life.
- maintaining a gratitude journal to habituate positivity.

Consider a firefighter who faces danger daily. They foster resilience by finding joy in the successful execution of their job and gratitude for the lives they save.

Growth Mindset: Learning in the Face of Challenges

A growth mindset is another robust strategy to build mental toughness. It involves viewing challenges as opportunities for learning rather than threats and embracing the potential for growth and improvement.

To cultivate a growth mindset, self-awareness about your self-talk and belief system is essential. Challenging self-defeating thoughts and reframing them positively fosters a growth mindset. A student struggling with complex math problems, for instance, can shift from feeling defeated to seeing the situation as an opportunity to learn and grow.

Stress Management: Mastering Your Response

Stress management is vital to building mental toughness. You can control stress by altering the stressful situation, changing your response to the situation, or finding ways to care for your emotional and physical health. Proven techniques include deep breathing, mindfulness, yoga, and regular exercise (Chen et al., 2015).

Living With Purpose: Aligning Actions With Values

A purpose in life, or a clear understanding of what truly matters to you, is a significant predictor of mental toughness. Identifying your passion and what you are willing to struggle for can help align your actions with your values, thereby enhancing mental toughness. For example, a social worker may face emotional strain, but their clear purpose of helping others keeps them mentally tough.

The Benefits of Mental Toughness

Boosting performance is one of the many advantages of mental toughness, as reinforced by a thorough review by Gucciardi et al. (2015). They scrutinized studies from sports, business, and educational arenas, all pointing toward a positive relationship between mental toughness and performance outcomes. Whether you're meeting a deadline at work, striving for academic excellence, or aspiring for athletic triumphs, mental toughness fuels success. It furnishes the mental endurance needed to sustain focus, overcome hurdles, and rebound from setbacks. This psychological robustness ensures optimal performance, regardless of the adversities faced.

Stress Resilience: A Byproduct of Mental Toughness

Research by Siddle et al. (2009) underscores the significance of mental toughness in managing stress. Those with higher levels of mental toughness interpret stressful situations as less threatening, exerting more control over their responses. These individuals maintain their poise, making effective decisions irrespective of the pressure they face. In a world where stress is a constant companion, mental toughness bestows you with the skills to cope, thereby promoting mental health and overall well-being.

Overcoming Limiting Beliefs Through Mental Toughness

Crust and Azadi (2010) highlight the correlation between mental toughness and the capacity to challenge self-imposed limitations. Individuals with high mental toughness harness positive cognitive strategies, such as constructive self-talk and visualization, to break free from the shackles of self-doubt. Instead of being deterred by the fear of failure, they perceive obstacles as growth opportunities. Essentially, mental toughness erects a psychological shield against limiting beliefs, liberating individuals to tap into their full potential.

Emotional Intelligence and Self-Belief: The Extended Benefits of Mental Toughness

Apart from enhancing performance and managing stress, mental toughness contributes to positive personal and interpersonal dynamics. It reinforces principles of emotional intelligence, fostering an unshakeable sense of self-belief. These attributes, in turn, can elevate overall life satisfaction and enhance relationships, stimulating a cycle of continued personal growth.

Resilience, a cornerstone of mental toughness, equips individuals to navigate life's vicissitudes more efficiently. They remain calm during crises, seeing challenges as transitory hurdles rather than impassable obstacles. This perspective fosters proactive problem-solving instead of denial or avoidance. It gives individuals the courage to confront difficulties and the resilience to recover from setbacks.

The influence of mental toughness on interpersonal relationships can't be overlooked. Those with high mental toughness exhibit emotional control, leading to improved communication and empathy. They manage complex conversations without losing their cool and empathize without being overwhelmed by emotions. This ability paves the way for effective communication, conflict resolution, and stronger relationships.

Mental toughness also gives birth to a robust sense of self-belief. Mentally tough individuals possess firm faith in their abilities and the confidence to chase their goals, unswayed by external judgment. This self-assurance is far from arrogance; it is a grounded belief in their capability, intertwined with the understanding that there's always room for growth. This blend of self-belief and humility fosters a continuous desire for self-improvement, steering individuals toward personal and professional milestones.

5B. CASE STUDIES OF MENTAL TOUGHNESS

Malala Yousafzai: Beacon of Resilience and Advocacy

At the heart of our exploration of mental toughness is Malala Yousafzai. As a young girl, she stood against the Taliban, advocating for girls' education in Pakistan. She showed exceptional courage and resilience, surviving an assassination attempt and leveraging her global platform to continue her advocacy. Yousafzai's profound statement, "One child, one teacher, one book, one pen can change the world," is a testament to her unyielding spirit. Her journey epitomizes the power of resilience and courage amidst extreme adversity.

Serena Williams: Testament for Resilience in Sports

Transitioning to the sports arena, we find Serena Williams, a tennis legend. Williams' journey is riddled with obstacles relating to gender, race, and health, yet she continuously demonstrates resilience, grit, and dedication. Her ethos, "I really think a champion is defined not by their wins but by how they can recover when they fall", exemplifies her resilience and highlights the essence of mental toughness in overcoming setbacks.

Stephen Hawking: Defying Physical Limitations With Mental Might

Stephen Hawking's life presents a compelling study of mental toughness. Diagnosed with a rare form of motor neuron disease at an early age, he didn't allow physical limitations to restrict his intellectual prowess. His mantra, "However difficult life may seem, there is always something you can do and succeed at," encapsulates his tenacious spirit and determination to contribute to science, regardless of the odds.

Maya Angelou: Rising Above Challenges With the Power of Words

The world of literature offers us Maya Angelou's inspiring life story. Despite her challenging upbringing marked by racial discrimination and personal trauma, Angelou demonstrated mental toughness by transforming her past into a source of inspiration. Her words, "You may not control all the events that happen to you, but you can decide not to be reduced by them," echo her resilient spirit, under-lining her determination to rise above her circumstances.

Nelson Mandela: Unyielding Resolve in the Face of Injustice

Nelson Mandela, the former South African President and a key figure in the struggle against apartheid, is a prime example of mental toughness. Despite 27 years in prison, Mandela remained resolute, playing a pivotal role in dismantling apartheid. His belief, "The greatest glory in living lies not in never falling, but in rising every time we fall," emphasizes his resilient spirit and belief in persistence.

Oprah Winfrey: From Rags to Riches, a Journey of Resilience

Next, we examine Oprah Winfrey, a name synonymous with success. From experiencing an impoverished childhood to becoming one of the world's most influential women, Winfrey's journey highlights her resilience and determination. Her philosophy, "The biggest adventure you can take is to live the life of your dreams," embodies the essence of mental toughness—embracing challenges and persisting until you reach your goals.

Elon Musk: Embodying Innovation and Risk-Taking

Finally, we examine Elon Musk, founder of several revolutionary companies like Tesla Motors and SpaceX. Known for his audacious visions, Musk's journey is punctuated by both failures and grand successes. Musk's ethos, "When something is important enough, you do it even if the odds are not in your favor," reflects his unwavering commitment to his goals, demonstrating resilience in adversity.

These diverse narratives, each serving as a beacon of mental toughness, demonstrate that overcoming limiting beliefs and reaching full potential is indeed possible, irrespective of the adversities one faces.

5C. STRATEGIES FOR DEVELOPING MENTAL TOUGHNESS

Developing mental toughness is akin to embarking on a journey filled with both challenges and opportunities for growth. The first obstacle often encountered is the fear of failure. This fear can act as a deterrent, discouraging us from taking risks or seeking out challenges due to the anxiety associated with making mistakes and the potential negative repercussions that may follow. A significant step to overcoming this fear is to change your perception of failure itself. Instead of seeing failure as an indication of inadequacy or weakness, you must reframe it as a catalyst for growth and learning. It is essential to recognize that mistakes provide opportunities to refine your strategies and improve your approaches. Every misstep brings you one step closer to success, and each failure adds to your reservoir of experience and knowledge.

Battling Self-Doubt

When you embrace failure as an integral part of the journey toward mental toughness, you open yourself to invaluable lessons and insights that you wouldn't have gained otherwise. As human beings, we often grapple with self-doubt, which can significantly impede our progress toward mental toughness. This lack of self-belief and confidence in your abilities can lead to procrastination, demotivation, and even self-sabotage. To overcome self-doubt, it becomes crucial to foster a sense of self-worth and confidence. This can be achieved by regularly practicing self-affirmation, seeking constructive feedback, setting achievable goals, and actively challenging negative self-talk with positive reinforcement.

Managing Setbacks and Difficulties

Acknowledging your feelings, practicing self-compassion, and externalizing how you feel are also critical steps in this process. This proactive approach aids in dismantling self-doubt and lays a strong foundation for the development of mental toughness. It is important to understand that the journey toward mental toughness is not a straight line. It is filled with ups and downs, moments of progress, and periods of setbacks. These instances should not be seen as signs of failure but rather as opportunities to exercise and bolster your mental toughness. They offer opportunities to apply the strategies and tools learned and to navigate through hardships with resilience and grit.

Maintaining Emotional Balance

Through moments of adversity, we can grow and strengthen mental fortitude. Building mental toughness is not about suppressing emotions or adopting a stoic facade. Rather, it's about fostering resilience and adaptability and maintaining a positive mindset amidst adversity. Mental toughness involves cultivating emotional balance, which means recognizing, acknowledging, and managing your emotions effectively. Connecting with others who support your journey, maintaining a hopeful outlook, and taking care of yourself physically and emotionally are integral to this process.

Embracing Change

Another common roadblock in the journey toward mental toughness is resistance to change. We humans are habitual creatures, and the idea of altering long-standing habits can be intimidating. However, developing mental toughness necessitates confronting these fears and embracing uncertainty. Overcoming resistance involves understanding the source of your fears, reframing change as an opportunity rather than a threat, visualizing the desired outcome, and taking small, manageable steps toward change. By doing so, you can gradually overcome resistance and make the process of cultivating mental toughness more accessible and less daunting.

Cultivating a Growth Mindset

Nurturing a growth mindset is crucial for mental toughness— it helps you believe that abilities can be developed through dedication and hard work. With a growth mindset, feelings of helplessness that often accompany obstacles can be effectively combated, thus fostering resilience and enhancing mental toughness. This mindset also encourages you to keep things in perspective and persist in the face of adversity.

The Continuous Journey of Mental Toughness

Developing mental toughness is not a one-time event. It is about relentlessly pursuing growth and improvement and viewing every challenge as an opportunity. Remember, on this journey, you're not alone. This book, your allies, and your internal fortitude are your guides, supporting you every step of the way on your path toward mental toughness.

5D: 10 EXERCISES TO BUILD MENTAL TOUGHNESS

Strengthening mental toughness and resilience is an ongoing process that can be fostered through daily exercise. Building these skills can often start with challenges that push you out of your comfort zone.

Exercise 1: Take cold showers. While initially uncomfortable, this practice will not only invigorate your senses but also allow you to embrace discomfort and exercise control over your reactions. Over time, this can enhance your ability to handle stress and adversity, contributing to mental toughness.

Exercise 2: Wait a few minutes before you eat when you're hungry. While it sounds simple, this activity is a test of patience and self-control. It encourages you to differentiate between your needs and wants, fostering a sense of discipline and self-restraint.

Exercise 3: Do what you least want to do. Dedicating even a little time, say ten minutes, to a task you've been avoiding or dreading, can help you face your fears or reluctance. This not only helps overcome procrastination but also strengthens your resilience to confront challenging tasks.

Exercise 4: Work out without distractions like music or television can be an effective exercise. This practice requires a high level of focus and self-discipline. It provides an opportunity to concentrate on your thoughts and feelings, fostering mindfulness and mental endurance.

Exercise 5: Acknowledge and sit with your feelings, regardless of whether they cause discomfort. This practice helps you become more aware of your emotional states and enhances your ability to manage and regulate emotions effectively.

Exercise 6: Identify and label your emotions. This can go hand in hand with the process above. After you sit with your emotions, label them like they are a science project. This exercise can help you gain clarity and control over your emotional responses, allowing you to navigate challenging situations with greater resilience. When you can name your feelings, you'll better understand what they are, why you feel them, and how you can process them while staying emotionally healthy.

Exercise 7: Focus on your breath. Deep breathing exercises play a significant role in developing mental toughness. By focusing on your breath, you can not only reduce stress and anxiety but also increase your awareness and focus. Deep breathing provides a sense of calm and clarity that helps with decision-making and emotional regulation.

Exercise 8: Voice your feelings. Having honest conversations with others is another useful exercise. Talking about your feelings, fears, and aspirations with someone you trust can provide emotional relief and a fresh perspective. It will help you articulate your thoughts, understand your emotions better, and gather support and encouragement.

Exercise 9: Appreciate what you have. Practicing gratitude is also an effective way to build mental toughness. By appreciating what you have, you culti-vate a positive mindset. This outlook can help you navigate life's challenges with more grace and resilience.

Exercise 10: Admit your mistakes. This is a crucial step toward building mental toughness. Accepting your faults instead of ignoring or denying them helps you learn and grow. It also fosters humility, a growth mindset, and the courage to take responsi-bility for your actions.

Incorporating these daily exercises into your routine can significantly enhance mental toughness and resilience over time. Each of these practices will push you to step out of your comfort zone, face your fears, and embrace growth, thereby fostering mental toughness and resilience.

5E. INTERACTIVE ELEMENT

Mental toughness, a fusion of resilience and well-being, can be fostered through interventions grounded in positive psychology. Let's explore a variety of simple yet effective exercises that can become a staple in your daily routine.

The Power of Mindfulness Meditation

A popular practice with demonstrated stress-reducing benefits is mindfulness meditation. By cultivating an awareness of the present, this practice enables you to explore your thoughts and feelings without judgment. Consider this a tool for mitigating negative emotions and disempowering beliefs. An accessible example is a five-minute meditation focusing on your breath. Maintain awareness of your breathing without attempting to control it. If your mind wanders, gently bring your attention back to your breath. Through regular practice, this exercise can enhance your ability to cope with stress and adversity.

Embracing Gratitude: The Path to Positive Mindset

Another tool for fortifying mental toughness is gratitude journaling, known to boost happiness and even improve physical health. Spend a few moments each day writing down three things you are grateful for. These can be simple joys like a comforting cup of coffee or a catch-up call with a friend. This practice can redirect your focus from scarcity to abundance, fostering a healthier mindset.

We often forget to acknowledge our personal strengths and achievements. Recognizing these can reinforce self-esteem, boost confidence, pave the way to resilience, and ultimately, empower you to confront challenges without faltering.

Grounded in positive psychology, the activity of reclaiming your strengths involves active reflection on your abilities and past successes. Positive psychology asserts that focusing on your strengths rather than your weaknesses and appreciating what is right with you rather than what is wrong can lead to increased happiness and fulfillment.

Strength Identification

To start, dedicate some quiet time to listing your personal strengths. These strengths can be various traits, talents, or skills you possess. Are you empathetic and able to understand and share the feelings of others? Are you resourceful and capable of overcoming difficulties in clever ways? Or perhaps you're a good listener or an excellent communicator. Whatever these strengths might be, recognizing them can help reinforce a positive self-image.

Reflecting on Triumphs

Once you've identified your strengths, turn your attention to instances in your past when you've utilized these strengths successfully. Reflecting on your triumphs, no matter how big or small, can be a major source of motivation and encouragement. They serve as proof of your capabilities, enhancing your belief in your ability to overcome future challenges.

To maximize the effectiveness of this resilience-building activity, consider incorporating it into your regular journaling practice. Here are five journal prompts that can guide you:

1. Strengths Exploration: "What personal strengths or unique skills do I possess? How have these strengths served me in the past?"

2. Victory Chronicle: "In what situation did I successfully use my strengths? How did it make me feel?"

3. Future Application: "How can I leverage my identified strengths to help me in my current or future challenges?"

4. Strengths Appreciation: "How can I celebrate and cultivate these strengths further?"

5. Daily Strengths Tracker: "How did I use my strengths today? How did it influence my experiences?"

Engaging in this resilience-building activity can help you reclaim your strengths, foster self-confidence, and enhance your capacity to navigate life's hurdles effectively. Harnessing the power within is the key to resilience and ultimately, mental toughness.

Daily Self-Reflection: The Path to Self-Awareness

Practicing self-reflection daily promotes self-awareness, which is a key to overcoming limiting beliefs. Dedicate a few minutes each day to review your thoughts, feelings, and behaviors. Reflect on what you've learned, areas of improvement, and your resilience. Recognizing these patterns will help you effectively identify and challenge limiting beliefs.

Finally, remember that patience and compassion toward yourself are paramount as you engage in these practices. Developing mental toughness is not about eliminating self-doubt or challenges, it's about your reaction to these experiences.

5F. KEY TAKEAWAYS

In conclusion, this chapter focuses on the immense potential of mental toughness as a tool for over-coming limiting beliefs. We have uncovered the foundational elements of mental toughness, from resilience and positivity to emotional regulation and mindfulness. These elements form a powerful toolkit that can help you face and overcome your limiting beliefs and enable you to navigate life's chal-lenges with grace and courage.

We also delved into the role of positivity in fostering mental toughness, acknowledging that maintaining a positive outlook isn't about ignoring difficulties but about choosing to focus on possibilities rather than constraints. Moreover, we've highlighted emotional regulation as an important skill to manage impulsive feelings that may arise when challenging your limiting beliefs. By learning to effectively handle these emotions, you can prevent them from hindering your progress.

On your journey to personal transformation, it's critical to recognize that mental toughness is more than just tenacity; it's a diverse set of skills that equip you to deal with life's challenges. These skills include

- Resilience
- Positivity
- Emotional control
- Mindfulness

Next, we'll look at personality changes where we'll debunk the myth that personality is unchangeable and demonstrate that it is a dynamic aspect of identity that can change over time.

6

UPGRADE YOURSELF

Have you ever wondered if you're truly capable of changing who you are? Do you feel trapped by the personality traits you were born with, or do you believe that you have the power to transform yourself into the person you want to be? The title of this chapter may prompt you to envision a high-tech science fiction scenario where humans merge with machines for a superhuman future. But in reality, "upgrading yourself" is an everyday, human endeavor. It involves reshaping your mind, broadening your perspective, and refining your skills to evolve into a better version of yourself. Each day presents an opportunity to learn, grow, and *upgrade* to become more resilient, more fulfilled, and better equipped to navigate the ups and downs of life.

Life is not a straight path with a predetermined endpoint but a continuous journey of discovery and transformation. And you are not merely a passenger on this journey but the driver. *You* have the power to influence the path you take on your journey; upgrade your mindset, skills, and behaviors; and craft a life that aligns with your values, passions, and purpose.

Consider this: Our smartphones and gadgets require regular updates and upgrades to function optimally. They need to adapt to the latest software, fix any bugs, and improve their overall performance. As humans, we too can benefit from regular upgrades. to continually learn and adapt, refine our skills, expand our knowledge, and improve our mindset so we can keep up with the ever-changing landscape of life.

You don't have to strive for perfection or compare yourself to others. Instead, recognize your potential for growth and take steps, however small, toward becoming the person you aspire to be. Learn from your experiences, embrace your strengths and weak-nesses, and transform challenges into opportunities for growth. When you cultivate a growth mindset, you view challenges as opportunities to learn and grow.

6A. ALL ABOUT YOUR PERSONALITY

Personality: A Unique Constellation of Traits That Define You

Our unique combinations of thoughts, feelings, behaviors, and experiences form the essence of who we are. Central to this singularity is personality—a constellation of enduring traits that influence how we think, feel, and behave across situations and over time. Let's delve into what forms this unique blend, starting with understanding what personality is and how it develops.

Decoding Personality: The Set of Traits That Define Us

Personality is a set of traits that are consistent over time and serve as the guiding light for your way of thinking, feeling, and behaving. These traits are not randomly assigned but are the result of a combination of several factors. They help you navigate through life, influence your interactions, and ultimately, weave the complex tapestry of your identity.

How is Personality Formed: The Interplay of Factors

Personality is not a monolith carved in stone. It is influenced and shaped by a multitude of factors including:

- Biological Factors: Genetics and brain structure contribute significantly to our personality formation with 40-60% of personality trait variations attributed to genetic influences (Mischel et al., 2008).
- Social Factors: Our cultural background, family environment, and interactions with others leave a lasting imprint on our personality.
- Psychological and Intellectual Factors: Our thoughts, emotions, experiences, intelligence, and cognitive abilities also play a vital role in shaping our personality.

The Fluid Nature of Personality: The Possibility of Change

Though our personality traits remain relatively stable, they aren't rigid. Research suggests that personalities can evolve throughout our lifespan, reflecting the changes that come with significant life events, intentional effort, or therapeutic interventions (Mõttus et al., 2017). This means that you can learn to manage or even change traits that don't align with your aspirations and values, underlining the fluid nature of personality.

Understanding that your personality is not static can be incredibly empowering. It challenges the common misconception that personality traits are like indelible ink tattoos on your psyche and opens the door to personal growth and self-improvement. The key to leveraging this fluidity lies in:

- Self-awareness: Identifying the traits you wish to modify or manage.
- Intentional effort: Proactively working toward influencing these traits.

That said, changing personality isn't simple. It requires persistence, patience, and sometimes professional guidance, especially given that these traits are deeply ingrained patterns of behavior, thinking, and feeling.

Such efforts can lead to substantial improvements in personal and professional life, overall well-being, and satisfaction. For instance, increasing conscientiousness can lead to better job performance and healthier habits, while enhancing emotional stability can result in lower stress levels and improved mental health.

Personality Traits and Life Choices: How They Interact

Your personality traits influence the decisions you make, often nudging you toward paths that resonate with your innate tendencies. For example, a person high in creativity may be drawn to pursuits or professions involving the arts or innovation and novelty. In contrast, highly extraverted individuals might find themselves thriving in social-interaction-heavy roles such as sales or public relations.

Freedom Beyond Traits: You're More Than Your Personality

While your traits can guide you, they do not determine your destiny. You hold the power to influence, manage, and even change these traits to align with your desired life outcomes. For instance, an introvert can cultivate social skills to excel in a career that demands high interpersonal interaction, despite their natural inclination for solitude.

The debate between nature and nurture is a long-standing discussion in the world of psychology that examines the extent to which certain aspects of our behavior are a product of either inherited genetic traits (nature) or our environment and experiences (nurture). When it comes to our personality traits and life choices, both of these elements come into play in a significant way.

Personality traits, many of which are believed to be largely determined by genetics, do indeed influence our decisions and life paths. Traits such as openness, conscientiousness, extraversion, agreeableness, and neuroticism—collectively known as the "Big Five" traits—have been shown to impact various areas of life, from career choices to relationships.

Understanding the Big Five Personality Traits

The Five-Factor Model, commonly known as the Big Five, provides a comprehensive framework for understanding personality. These traits, in various combinations, help define our personalities and significantly influence our behavior. For instance, someone high in conscientiousness would likely be punctual and organized, while someone high in extraversion might find themselves being more sociable and outgoing.

Openness

Openness to experience reflects your willingness to embrace new experiences and your capacity for creativity, imagination, and intellectual curiosity. The adventurous souls scoring high in openness thrive when exploring unfamiliar terrains, indulging their imagination, and seeking out knowledge. In contrast, individuals scoring low appreciate the comfort of familiarity and routine.

Conscientiousness

Conscientiousness essentially measures your organizational skills, dependability, and discipline. If meticulous planning, attention to detail, and punctuality are your traits, you score high in conscientiousness. Conversely, low scorers find joy in spontaneity, flexibility, and improvisation and often find stringent structures suffocating.

Extraversion

Extraversion represents your sociability, assertiveness, and capacity for experiencing positive emotions. High scorers, typically outgoing and expressive, revel in social interactions and become the heart and soul of any gathering. Lower scorers, while no less sociable, prefer quieter, more intimate interactions and find solace in solitude.

Agreeableness

Agreeableness uncovers your compassion, cooperativeness, and likability. High scorers, empathetic and conflict-averse individuals, often prioritize harmonious relationships over their needs. Low scorers, while not necessarily disagreeable, value constructive conflict and stand their ground assertively.

Neuroticism

Neuroticism assesses your emotional stability and responses to stress. High scorers are susceptible to worries and stress and feel a wide range of emotions intensely. Conversely, individuals scoring low on neuroticism demonstrate emotional resilience, remain calm under pressure, and recover rapidly from negative emotions.

On the one hand, individuals high in openness, characterized by curiosity, creativity, and a preference for novelty and variety, may be more inclined toward professions that allow them to explore new ideas and think outside the box—art, research, or entrepreneurship. On the other hand, individuals high in extraversion, characterized by outgoingness, sociability, and assertiveness, may be naturally drawn to roles that involve a great deal of social interaction—sales, marketing, or public relations.

Despite the influence of these innate tendencies on our decisions and life paths, we are not bound by our personality traits. "Nature" does not dictate our destiny. This is where "nurture" comes into play. Our environment, experiences, and deliberate choices can shape our personality and behavior, sometimes counteracting or enhancing our natural tendencies.

An introvert, for example, may be inclined to solitude and find social situations draining. However, this doesn't mean that they cannot succeed in a career that requires high levels of interpersonal interaction. Through deliberate practice and exposure, they can cultivate the social skills necessary to excel in such a role. This is a testament to the power of a growth mindset. Instead of viewing personality traits as fixed and unchangeable, a growth mindset recognizes the capacity for change and development.

In fact, research in the field of personality psychology supports this idea. While our traits do exhibit a certain degree of stability over time, they are not set in stone. Our personality can and does change over the course of our lives, influenced by our experiences, our environment, and our conscious efforts. This underscores the idea that you are more than your personality traits and that you have the capacity to shape your own path, regardless of your natural inclinations.

The idea of personality fluidity breaks the mold of the traditional belief that personalities are immovable. By acknowledging that you can influence and change personality traits, you unlock the doors to personal growth and self-improvement.

Therefore, while the nature vs. nurture debate offers valuable insights into the origins and development of personality, perhaps the most important takeaway is the understanding that you are not a mere product of your genetics or environment. You are an active agent in your own life, capable of growth, change, and self-determination. By embracing this perspective, you are better equipped to cultivate a growth mindset and navigate the journey toward your desired outcomes.

Understanding and Accepting: The Cornerstones of Change

The first step to changing your personality is to understand and accept yourself. Start by identifying the traits that serve you and the ones that hinder you. With this self-awareness, you can take proactive steps to manage or even change these traits to align more closely with your life goals.

Each small step toward understanding and modifying your personality traits is a leap toward personal growth. While change can feel daunting, remember that it's a journey, not a destination. With knowledge, openness, and the understanding that change is within your grasp, let's embark on this journey together.

To begin this process, journaling can be an immensely helpful tool. Here are some prompts designed to facilitate self-understanding and self-acceptance:

1. Personal Trait Analysis: Spend some time introspecting your personality traits. Write them down, both the ones you consider positive and those you view as negative. For each trait, provide a detailed example of

when it was particularly noticeable. Reflect on how these traits influenced the situation and your reaction to it.

2. Focusing on Strengths: Choose three traits from your list that you identify as personal strengths. Elaborate on how these strengths have helped you in your personal and professional life. Write about specific instances where these traits empowered you to overcome challenges or achieve your goals. How can you continue to harness these strengths moving forward?

3. Work Through Challenges: Select three traits from your list that you perceive as obstacles or areas of improvement. Describe in detail the challenges you face due to these traits. Write about specific situations where these traits might have held you back or caused difficulties. It's essential to approach this exercise with compassion and understanding.

4. Embracing Self-Acceptance: For each trait you identified as challenging, write a self-compassionate paragraph accepting that trait as part of your current self. You don't have to like it or resign yourself to it but

rather acknowledge its presence. How does accepting this trait change your perspective about yourself and your potential for growth?

5. Mapping the Journey to Change: Take each challenging trait and map out a detailed plan to manage or change this trait so it aligns better with your life goals. Include small, achievable steps, and focus on practical actions. Also, write about how these changes would help you grow, using specific examples of potential future situations.

6B. UPGRADING TO YOUR BEST SELF

Personality and personal growth are closely intertwined, shaping and influencing each other in a continuous feedback loop. This interaction sets the stage for your life journey, influencing your career, relationship, and even worldview. Understanding this interaction can provide critical insights into how you can leverage personality traits for enhanced personal growth.

Traits such as conscientiousness and openness to experience, for example, can enhance goal-oriented behavior and intellectual growth, respectively.

However, unbalanced traits can hinder your growth trajectory—excessive conscientiousness may stifle creativity, and extreme openness can lead to a lack of focus and instability.

The Power of Change: Your Personality Isn't Set in Stone

A potential for change is the fundamental tenet of our personalities. Our traits aren't rigid structures but rather dynamic and evolving entities that can be molded to facilitate our personal growth.

For example, if you identify as highly impulsive, developing strategies to manage impulsiveness can lead to better decisions. Similarly, if you are an introvert, working on enhancing extraversion could significantly improve your social interactions.

This process of evolution isn't about discarding your core self or imitating someone else. It's about refining and managing your traits in ways that align with your personal growth goals and your true self.

Change as a Catalyst for Personal Growth

Deliberate personality change can unlock immense personal growth potential. When you choose to modify your traits, you not only alter your behaviors but also restructure your perceptions and responses, paving the way for profound personal growth.

Consider someone who struggles with low conscientiousness and finds it hard to maintain routines or fulfill responsibilities. Deliberately increasing conscientiousness can help them enhance productivity. Similarly, for someone with high neuroticism, working toward emotional stability can greatly enhance mental health and resilience, thus setting the stage for long-term personal growth.

Remember, you're not trying to achieve an ideal personality, you're fostering a personality that best facilitates your growth and well-being. It's about acknowledging and honoring yourself, while also identifying areas for improvement.

Personality traits, their changes, and the resulting personal growth form a complex and dynamic interplay. Recognizing this interaction and leveraging it to our advantage can harness the power of your personality to achieve your aspirations and foster a fulfilling and authentic life.

While this journey requires self-awareness, effort, and sometimes, professional support, the rewards are immense and can transform your life in profound and enduring ways. Embracing the power to change can unlock the potential for remarkable personal growth, leading to a journey that is as fulfilling as the destination.

The Profound Impact of Intentional Change

Bringing about intentional change to personality is not about altering your behavior but rather altering your perceptions and responses to the world around you. The effects of this reshaping can have profound implications for personal growth. It enables you to achieve your goals, improve your relationships, and lead a more fulfilling life.

Let's illustrate this point with an example. If you find yourself constantly struggling with your responsibilities, intentionally enhance conscientiousness to boost your productivity and reliability. This shift will not only enhance your current circumstances but also pave the way for long-term personal growth.

Shaping Your Destiny: The Power of Change

Ultimately, personal growth and personality are two sides of the same coin. Our personalities can influence our growth trajectories, and vice versa. The conscious decision to refine and manage your personality traits can significantly reshape your life paths, allowing you to harness the power of change to foster personal growth.

Embrace the power of change and leverage it to mold your personality in a way that supports your growth, enhances your relationships, and improves your life.

The power to shape your destiny and foster a fulfilling and authentic life that reflects your true self lies with you. Harness it to fuel personal growth.

Charting Your Own Course: Identifying Traits for Development

Armed with self-awareness, you can pinpoint specific traits you want to refine or augment. Remember, your choices should resonate with your goals and values, regardless of external expectations or societal norms. You don't need to fit into a specific mold but bolster an authentic version of yourself.

Laying the Foundation: Goal Setting and Strategy Development

With your target traits identified, it's time to establish SMART goals. For example, to nurture a sense of extraversion, you could aim to "Initiate two new conversations every week for the next two months."

Self-reflection: The Compass of Change

Having set your goals, the journey truly begins. Self-reflection allows you to routinely assess your progress, understand any roadblocks, and if necessary, refine your strategies. Tools like journaling and mindfulness exercises can significantly aid this process.

Embodying Change: Adopting New Behaviors

The time has come to put your plans into action. Depending on the goals you've identified, adopt new behaviors that align with your targets. This could range from fostering resilience by adopting stress management techniques to enhancing emotional stability by practicing calming exercises. Remember, consistency is key, and with time, these new behaviors will become a part of your fabric.

The Power of Patience and Persistence

Progress in areas of self-development is often slow and incremental. Embrace this process and remember, it's perfectly normal to stumble along the way. Each falter is not a failure but an opportunity for growth and learning. Each step forward, no matter how tiny, is progress. Celebrating these small victories will not only fuel your motivation but also reinforce your commitment to the journey.

Taking Baby Steps: The Importance of Starting Small

Developing new behaviors might seem challenging, especially if they significantly differ from our current ones. But remember the power of small, manageable changes. You don't have to leap out of your comfort zone all at once, gradual steps are equally impactful.

The concept of taking baby steps underscores the importance of starting small when it comes to habit formation or personal development. Making small, manageable changes can lead to substantial, long-lasting progress over time. Here are a few examples of how you might take baby steps in different areas:

1. Exercising: If you want to adopt a more active lifestyle but don't currently engage in regular physical activity, a baby step might be to start with just five minutes of exercise per day. You could walk around your block, do some light stretching, or even dance to

your favorite song. Gradually, increase the duration and intensity of your workouts.

2. Eating Healthy: If you want to improve your diet, a baby step would be adding an extra serving of vegetables to your dinner each night or replacing one sugary drink with a glass of water each day. Over time, these small changes can lead to healthier eating habits.

3. Practicing Mindfulness: If you'd like to be more mindful or present, start with just two minutes of meditation each day. Over time, slowly increase the duration as you become more comfortable with the practice.

4. Reading: If you want to read more but struggle to find time, start with just five minutes of reading per day—you might do this before bed as a way to unwind. Gradually, increase this time as you get more engrossed in the habit of reading.

5. Cultivating a Growth Mindset: If you're working toward developing a growth mindset, a baby step could be reflecting on one failure or challenge each day and identifying what you learned from it. Over

time, this practice can help shift your perspective on failures and challenges.

Baby steps emphasize that progress is made up of small, steady steps. Each step, no matter how small, is a move in the right direction. Never underestimate the power of these small changes; they can add up to considerable progress over time.

Keep the Feedback Loop Active: Regular Self-Reflection

Incorporate self-reflection into your routine. Assess your progress, understand any challenges, and adjust your strategies as required. Journaling your thoughts and observations can be an invaluable tool here, providing valuable insights into your journey.

When cultivating a growth mindset, maintaining an active feedback loop through regular self-reflection is paramount. Self-reflection serves as a mirror, providing you with an opportunity to look at your actions, emotions, and progress objectively. It allows you to understand successes, challenges, and areas that require improvement or adjustment.

Self-reflection encourages introspection and fosters a deeper understanding of yourself, including your motivations, emotional responses, and behavioral patterns. By routinely examining your thoughts and actions, you create opportunities to celebrate progress, identify challenges or obstacles, and strategize how best to overcome them.

For instance, if you're working on becoming more patient, regular reflection can provide valuable insights. You might notice patterns in certain situations that particularly test your patience or recognize small victories when you were more patient than you would have been in the past.

Journaling is an excellent tool to facilitate this process. The act of writing not only helps you articulate your thoughts more clearly but also provides a tangible record of your growth journey.

To help you get started, here are five detailed journal prompts to foster regular self-reflection:

1. Reflecting on Progress: Write about your journey toward adopting a growth mindset over the past month. What are some significant changes you've noticed in your attitudes or behaviors? Provide specific examples. How do these changes make you feel?

2. Understanding Challenges: Reflect on the obstacles you faced while trying to incorporate a growth mindset. What were these challenges? How did you react to them? Was your response in line with the principles of a growth mindset?

3. Celebrating Victories: Identify and write about three instances where you successfully demonstrated a growth mindset. How did you feel during these instances? How did these successes impact your confidence in your ability to change and grow?

4. Adjusting Strategies: Consider any strategies you've been using to cultivate a growth mindset. Are there any that aren't working as well as you'd hoped? Why might this be? Write about how you could adjust these strategies to overcome the challenges you've identified.

5. Setting Future Goals: Reflect on your growth journey so far and look ahead to the future. What are some areas you'd like to focus on going forward? Set specific, achievable goals for these areas. Write about why these goals are important to you and how you plan to achieve them.

As you strive for change, expect moments of discomfort and resistance. Rather than signs of defeat, see them as growing pains. Treat these instances with compassion and learn from them, using each one as a stepping stone toward your goal.

6C. INTERACTIVE ELEMENT

Creating Your Personality Inventory

Now that we have a better understanding of the Big 5 personality traits, let's start creating our personality inventory. Remember, you're not looking to fit into categories but rather gain insights into your personality for self-improvement.

Rate Your Traits

Reflect on each trait and rate yourself on a scale of 1 to 10 for each one. Be honest and open—remember, this exercise is for your benefit and growth.

Consider:

- Openness: I eagerly embrace new ideas OR I prefer established routines.

- Conscientiousness: I am organized and detail oriented OR I thrive in spontaneous situations.
- Extraversion: I seek out social situations and enjoy engaging with others OR I value solitary time and intimate interactions.
- Agreeableness: I am naturally empathetic and cooperative OR I have a competitive edge and don't shy away from conflict.
- Neuroticism: I often succumb to worries OR I display emotional resilience under stress.

Identify Related Behaviors, Emotions, and Thoughts

To validate your ratings, identify specific behaviors, emotions, or thoughts aligned with your scores. If you've given yourself a high conscientiousness score, you might find evidence in your adherence to schedules or meticulousness. A low extraversion score could be reflected in your preference for solitude or small gatherings.

Reflect, Don't Judge

As you engage in this process, you might discover aspects of your personality that were previously hidden. Embrace these revelations as part of your growth journey. Refrain from judging or criticizing yourself; instead, view these traits as unique aspects of your identity.

Now that you've completed your personality inventory, take a moment to absorb this knowledge. This inventory serves as a snapshot of your current personality.

Reflect on Your Ratings

Alongside each rating, note down the reason for your scores. Pinpoint specific instances that back your ratings. This deepens self-awareness and lays the foundation for the changes you aim to make.

Here are five journal prompts to inspire reflections. These are based on taking small steps and assessing personal characteristics:

1. Reflecting With Baby Steps: Reflect on an area of your life where you would like to make a change. Identify one small, manageable step you could take toward this change. Why did you choose this step, and how do you think it will help you move toward your larger goal?
2. Analyzing Behavior: Think about your daily routine and habits. Identify one behavior

that you think reflects an aspect of your personality and write about why you believe this is the case. Remember, you're not judging your behavior, just understanding its connection to your actions and inner self.

3. Evaluating Emotions: Consider a recent emotional response you've had to a situation. Write about the emotions you experienced and why you think you felt that way. How does this emotional response align with your understanding of your personality?

4. Investigating Thoughts: Reflect on your thought patterns, especially those that occur regularly or automatically. Choose one recurring thought and write about how it might be linked to your personality traits.

5. Planning for Future Small Steps: Now that you've spent time reflecting on your behaviors, emotions, and thoughts, identify a small new step you'd like to take in the upcoming week that aligns with your goals. Write about why you chose this step and how you plan to incorporate it into your life.

This personal exercise may lead to profound revelations about your personality. While sharing your insights can be beneficial, consider keeping this inventory private for now to safeguard your reflections from external influences.

Your journey of personal growth is lifelong, and these ratings are not fixed. They may evolve over time, reflecting your growth and evolution. Revisit these journal prompts periodically to see how your traits morph over time, marking your progression toward your best self.

Cultivate an Objective Outlook

Throughout this process, it's essential to cultivate an objective view. If you find that you score high in neuroticism, for instance, avoid labeling it as bad. Instead, recognize it as a part of who you are at present. Each trait comes with its unique set of strengths and challenges; understanding these nuances will empower you to shape your growth journey more effectively.

Your traits are not rigid classifications but starting points for self-improvement. High conscientiousness may mean you're well-organized and responsible, but it can also mean that you are prone to perfectionism or inflexibility. Conversely, while low agreeableness may indicate a tendency for competitiveness, it also may mean that you're more willing to engage in difficult conversations and stand your ground when necessary.

Approach With Curiosity

Embrace a sense of curiosity when self-reflecting. Remember, traits are complex and multi-dimensional; a single trait can manifest differently in different people. Instead of viewing your scores as good or bad, think of them as pieces of yourself and indicators of potential growth. Armed with these insights, you're now ready to set out on your journey toward personal growth.

Your personality inventory is unique to you. It provides a starting point, a way for you to understand your present self and navigate toward your desired self. Progress at your own pace, keeping your unique personality constellation in mind.

Remember: It's a Marathon, Not a Sprint

Personal growth is not achieved overnight; it's a marathon that spans the course of your life. Your personality inventory will serve as a compass, guiding you on your journey. Keep it close, revisit it often, and let it illuminate your path as you navigate your way toward your best self.

In the end, understanding your personality traits is about understanding the unique blend of traits that make you who you are. It's about acknowledging your strengths, recognizing areas for growth, and setting out on your personal journey toward becoming your best self.

6D. KEY TAKEAWAYS

So far, we have examined the powerful role personality plays in shaping our experiences, behaviors, and interactions with the world around us. A variety of factors, from biological to psychological, weave together to form the vibrant tapestry of our personalities.

We dived into the Five-Factor Model, a comprehensive representation of personality traits that include openness, conscientiousness, extraversion, agreeableness, and neuroticism, each with its unique influence on our actions and decisions.

Contrary to popular belief, we discovered that our personalities are not set in stone and can evolve over time. This realization helped foster hope and provide a pathway for personal growth and transformation.

The importance and role of self-awareness in changing personality were highlighted. Several strategies were discussed, including identifying traits to change, setting realistic goals, practicing self-reflection, implementing new behaviors, and being patient and persistent.

We put theory into practice with a personality inventory exercise based on the Big Five personality traits, providing a clear picture of your current personality traits and a baseline for future self-improvement efforts.

Understanding your personality is crucial for overcoming limiting beliefs and propelling personal growth. Armed with this newfound knowledge, you're now ready to take definitive steps toward becoming the best version of yourself.

7

UNLOCK YOUR POTENTIAL

A t the heart of this exploration lies a simple but profound truth: change is possible, and the capacity for personal growth is limitless. When we believe that our potential is not fixed but a pliable construct that can be nurtured and expanded, we can continually learn, adapt, and improve our abilities. As such, a growth mindset becomes the key that can unlock abundant opportunities, serving as the catalyst for unprecedented personal and professional success.

To encapsulate the spirit of this journey, consider this poignant quote from renowned inventor Thomas A. Edison, "I have not failed. I've just found 10,000 ways that won't work". Edison's words echo the essence of a growth mindset, reflecting the belief that failure is not a dead end but rather a stepping stone toward success, a necessary part of the learning process. This resilient attitude transforms obstacles into opportunities, fostering resilience and promoting personal growth.

7A. DEVELOPING A GROWTH MINDSET

A growth mindset, introduced by psychologist Carol Dweck, is the belief that our skills and intelligence can be honed through dedication, education, and perseverance. This perspective encourages growth and evolution (emphasizing effort as the avenue to expertise) and the acceptance of trials and setbacks as integral parts of the journey to mastery.

Personal and Professional Implications of a Growth Mindset

Adopting a growth mindset paves the way for opportunities, resilience, and lifelong learning, fostering adaptive behaviors that support success. Let's explore these benefits in detail:

- Enhancing self-esteem: A growth mindset perceives abilities as flexible and helps you maintain high self-esteem, even when faced with setbacks.
- Acquiring new skills: Your conviction in your ability to learn and refine fuels the procurement of novel skills and knowledge.
- Embracing challenges: With a growth mindset, you're more likely to perceive challenges as growth opportunities, stimulating personal and professional development.

A Practical Example

Consider someone who's struggling with a sophisticated skill like programming. If they have a fixed mindset, they might surrender, believing they lack the natural talent for it. Conversely, someone with a growth mindset would acknowledge the complexity of the skill that they are trying to develop and continue practicing tenaciously.

Resilience and Growth: The Perfect Symbiosis

Resilience, or the ability to swiftly recover from difficulties, is closely tied to a growth mindset. By embracing challenges and failures as learning experiences, a growth mindset enhances resilience, helping individuals rebound from adversities and continue their pursuit of growth. It also nurtures a love for learning and acceptance of failure, fostering a resilience that is crucial for achieving long-term goals.

Resilience and a growth mindset are both linked to positivity and optimism. While resilience enables you to maintain a positive view even under trying circumstances, a growth mindset develops a positive conviction in the possibilities for change and growth. This optimistic outlook promotes improved emotional well-being, problem-solving skills, and the capacity to stay motivated and laser-focused on long-term objectives.

Unlocking Boundless Potential With a Growth Mindset

A growth mindset cultivates an inner environment conducive to constant learning and improvement, thus allowing you to frequently embrace new challenges and see them not as overwhelming obstacles but as opportunities for growth. By doing so, you uncover the vast potential within yourself, nurtured through diligence and perseverance.

Learning From Criticism: The Growth Mindset Approach

A growth mindset builds a framework that welcomes feedback. It encourages you to perceive criticism not as a personal attack but as a tool for improvement, paving the way for personal and professional development.

Resilience and a growth mindset form a formidable strategy to combat limiting beliefs. By embracing the concept of growth and fostering resilience, you can dismantle these barriers, transforming challenges into opportunities for growth.

The Power of a Growth Mindset: Transcending Perceived Limitations

The strength of a growth mindset lies in its ability to transform perceived limitations into platforms for progress, unlocking the potential within you. Reflecting on this concept in real-world scenarios can further highlight the influence of a growth mindset.

Consider someone who's learning a new language or a musical instrument. With a fixed mindset, they might find the initial stages of learning and error daunting and surrender early, believing they lack innate talent. Conversely, someone with a growth mindset would recognize that initial failure is part of learning and continue putting in effort and practicing.

The combination of a growth mindset and resilience equips you with the necessary tools to navigate life's challenges and continue pursuing your goals.

In this light, it becomes clear that a growth mindset is not only about personal development but also about our interactions with others and the world around us. This worldview encourages us to

- Accept Constructive Criticism: A growth mindset will help you perceive feedback as an opportunity to grow and understand that constructive criticism can be a powerful agent for change and improvement.
- Develop Resilience: A growth mindset will empower you to bounce back from adversities quickly. It fosters the understanding that failure is not a stumbling block but a stepping stone toward success.
- Recognize and Harness Potential: A growth mindset helps you see that your talents and abilities are not limited and encourages you to appreciate and tap into your immense potential.

Reframing Challenges: The Role of a Growth Mindset

A crucial aspect of a growth mindset is the ability to reframe challenges. By viewing challenges as opportunities to learn and grow, you can transform your approach to problem-solving and decision-making.

Building Resilience Through a Growth Mindset

In addition to its powerful influence on personal growth, a growth mindset also plays a pivotal role in cultivating resilience. Resilience is bolstered by a growth mindset's inherent acceptance of challenges and failures as essential parts of the learning process, thus equipping you with the ability to weather life's storms and maintain a clear path toward your goals.

The Power of Transformation: Growth Mindset in Action

Embracing a growth mindset and fostering resilience can effectively dismantle the barriers constructed by limiting beliefs. These self-imposed constraints can cloud your perception of your abilities and potential, effectively preventing personal growth.

However, imbibing a growth mindset and developing resilience can break down these limitations, converting challenges into opportunities for growth and self-improvement. The power of a growth mindset lies in its ability to transform perceived limitations into launching pads for progress, unlocking the limitless potential within each one of us.

7B. USING A GROWTH MINDSET TO ACHIEVE PERSONAL AND PROFESSIONAL GOALS

A fundamental part of adopting a growth mindset is to embrace the learning process. You must value the journey of acquiring knowledge and skills over simply achieving an end goal and recognize that setbacks, challenges, and failures are natural and beneficial components of the learning process. By embracing this outlook, you don't just learn, you grow. You also learn to reflect on mistakes and setbacks, creating a loop of continuous learning and growth.

A sense of purpose is another crucial factor that can guide your journey to growth. Having a clear purpose helps to shape your actions, behaviors, and decisions. When you're clear about what you are striving for and why, the path to achieving your goals can become more manageable and focused. This sense of purpose becomes the driving force that propels you forward, especially in the face of challenges and adversity. Not only can this fuel your motivation, but it can also provide a sense of fulfillment and meaning in your life.

Adopting a positive attitude toward yourself and your capabilities is the cornerstone of a growth mindset. A positive attitude helps recognize and celebrate your strengths, as well as acknowledging areas where there is room for growth. When you cultivate a positive mindset, you build resilience, increase confidence, and march toward your goals.

Surrounding yourself with positive influences plays a significant role in promoting a growth mindset. Whom you choose to spend time with can impact your attitude, motivation, and outlook on life. By seeking out mentors, coaches, and other positive influences, you can find support, encouragement, and inspiration for your personal and professional goals. Moreover, individuals who embody a growth mindset can serve as living examples of how to overcome challenges, persist in the face of setbacks, and continuously strive for improvement.

When You Should Take Calculated Risks

Taking risks is part of growth. Stepping outside of your comfort zone allows you to tackle new challenges and grow from the experiences they provide. By taking calculated risks, you allow yourself to embrace uncertainty, make informed decisions, and continue learning, even when faced with potential failure.

Understanding Your Journey of Growth

Cultivating a growth mindset may initially feel daunting, as it can imply an incessant need for change and improvement. However, it is not about constant pressure to perform, but rather a compassionate understanding of your capabilities, your potential for growth, and the awareness that learning is a journey. Growing is all about allowing yourself the grace to learn, unlearn, and relearn and understanding that progress isn't linear.

For instance, when embracing the learning process, one important thing to bear in mind is that learning is not merely about acquiring knowledge but also about developing competencies and adapting to changes. This belief is instrumental in equipping you with the necessary tools to tackle the challenges you face and in encouraging you to seek knowledge beyond the confines of your current understanding.

7C: THE BLUEPRINT TO A GROWTH MINDSET

Recognizing Your Prevailing Mindset

The journey toward a growth mindset begins with the introspective task of identifying your own mindset. Reflect on your perspective of your abilities and the concept of intelligence. Do you see these as innate and unalterable? Or do you see them as malleable, capable of improvement with effort and learning? By recognizing these thought patterns, you initiate the shift from a fixed mindset to a growth mindset.

Consider a situation where you faced a significant challenge. If your immediate response was to avoid it due to fear of failure, this might suggest a fixed mindset. Conversely, if you saw the challenge as an opportunity to learn and grow, this indicates a growth mindset.

Tracking Your Progress

Identifying your mindset is the first step, and observing your progression is the second. Tracking your progress involves noting improvements in resilience, handling of setbacks, and reception to criticism. A growth mindset values the journey as much as the destination, placing equal emphasis on the learning process and the outcome.

Reflect on the previous month. Identify one instance where you responded more resiliently to a setback or criticism than before. It may be subtle, but this is a sign of growth and progress.

Learning From Others

Observing and learning from others' successes can be enlightening. Success is seldom a product of overnight effort; it typically involves consistent learning, adaptability, and perseverance. This understanding can serve as a roadmap and an inspirational guide in your journey to developing a growth mindset.

For example, think of a successful person in your life. Rather than simply acknowledging their success, try to understand the journey they undertook to get there—their trials, tribulations, and triumphs.

Embracing Constructive Feedback

Soliciting and embracing feedback is a crucial element in fostering a growth mindset. Feedback, when viewed through the lens of learning and growth rather than personal criticism, serves as a springboard for improvement.

Next time you receive feedback, try to look at it as a source of learning. Consider it an opportunity to understand different perspectives and identify areas of improvement.

Unlocking the Power of "Yet"

The word "yet" brings a future-oriented perspective to your abilities. Reframing your thoughts from "I can't do this" to "I can't do this yet" implies that with effort and time, you can acquire the necessary skills or knowledge. This linguistic shift can instill a sense of optimism and perseverance, both elements intrinsic to a growth mindset.

The next time you find yourself doubting your abilities, add the word 'yet' at the end of your thought. Notice how this subtle change can dramatically shift your perspective and motivation.

Stepping Out of Your Comfort Zone

The willingness to learn new things is instrumental in reinforcing a growth mindset. This process often requires stepping outside of your comfort zone, thereby strengthening the belief that abilities can be improved upon.

Challenge yourself to learn something new each week. It could be a new word, a fact about a different culture, or a new recipe.

Fostering a growth mindset often involves pushing yourself beyond the boundaries of your comfort zone. While staying within this zone can bring feelings of security and routine, it often also results in stagnation, lack of creativity, and limited personal and professional growth. In contrast, stepping outside your comfort zone exposes you to new experiences and challenges that can foster growth, learning, and improvement.

Cultivating a willingness to learn new things is instrumental in stepping out of the comfort zone. When you open yourself up to new experiences, you essentially expand your horizons and create more opportunities for growth.

By consciously making the decision to learn something new each week, you actively choose to grow. Whether it's a new word in a different language, an interesting fact about another culture, a new recipe, or a new skill entirely, each new piece of knowledge you acquire is a step toward personal growth.

Moreover, the act of consistently learning something new, even if it's small, strengthens your belief in the potential for improvement. It serves as a constant reminder that abilities and skills are not fixed and can be developed and refined over time.

Here are some related journal prompts that can help you step out of your comfort zone:

1. Write about a time when you stepped out of your comfort zone. What did you learn from this experience?
2. Describe a skill or activity that lies outside of your comfort zone that you'd like to try. What steps can you take to begin this journey?
3. Reflect on any fears or reservations you might have about stepping out of your comfort zone. How can you address them?
4. Identify one new thing you'd like to learn this week. It could be a new word, a fact about a different culture, a new cooking recipe, etc.

5. At the end of each week, write about what you learned. How did it make you feel? What challenges did you face, and how did you overcome them?

The goal of these journal prompts isn't to prompt immediate, sweeping changes, but rather to encourage small, consistent steps toward embracing a growth mindset and stepping out of your comfort zone.

Reframing Mistakes as Learning Opportunities

The next time you make a mistake, instead of feeling defeated, ask yourself: "What can I learn from this experience?"

An integral aspect of a growth mindset is self-compassion. Growth is a journey marked by triumphs and setbacks. Being kind to yourself during this journey, particularly during the challenging phases, is crucial. Acknowledge that everyone makes mistakes and that it's okay to stumble. Mistakes are a natural part of the learning process. When a setback is encountered, instead of engaging in self-criticism, use it as an opportunity to practice self-compassion. Remind yourself that it's okay to not know everything and most importantly, that it's okay to be a work in progress.

A growth mindset also recognizes that the road to improvement and success is often marked with bumps and detours. While the journey may not always be easy, it's good to remember that growth is a process, not a destination. The path to mastery is rarely a straight line; it's more akin to a winding road with ups and downs. Along this road, there will be moments of triumph and moments of setback. A growth mindset encourages us to view these setbacks not as failures but as necessary and valuable components of the journey toward growth.

Adopting a growth mindset entails a comprehensive reframing of how we perceive and react to mistakes. It encourages us to view mistakes as teachers rather than indicators of failure. It promotes the understanding that growth is a journey that will inevitably involve setbacks. And perhaps most importantly, it underlines the necessity of treating yourself with compassion throughout the process as you continually strive to learn, improve, and grow.

Using Examples as a Catalyst for Growth

Examples serve as tangible proof that a growth mindset can lead to success. They can inspire and motivate you to embrace this mindset, whether they come from your personal experiences, people around you, or famous personalities.

For instance, consider the story of Thomas Edison. Despite numerous failures, his persistent attitude ultimately led to his revolutionary invention—the electric light bulb.

Thomas Edison's life is a quintessential example of a growth mindset in action. His story is rich with instances of resilience, perseverance, and unwavering belief in his abilities, all of which are central to developing a growth mindset.

Known to many as one of the greatest inventors in history, Edison's journey was not a smooth ride. In fact, one of his most well-known endeavors, the invention of the electric light bulb, was born out of a relentless series of trials and errors. Rather than seeing his repeated unsuccessful attempts as failures, he chose to view them as stepping stones toward his ultimate goal. He viewed each setback as an opportunity to learn something new, to refine his process, and to inch one step closer to his eventual success.

Edison's commitment to continuous learning is another key aspect of his growth mindset. He had minimal formal education, but that did not deter him from acquiring knowledge in various fields. His thirst for knowledge was insatiable and lifelong. Edison firmly believed in the potential of hard work and effort to overcome barriers and achieve mastery.

In the face of criticism and skepticism, Edison held steadfast to his vision. When others doubted the feasibility of his ideas, he remained undeterred. This unshakeable belief in his vision, even when the odds seemed stacked against him, is another hallmark of a growth mindset. Edison did not allow the fear of failure or the judgments of others to dissuade him from pursuing his ambitions.

Finally, Edison's definition of success was intrinsically linked to his growth mindset. For him, success was not simply about achieving a desired outcome but also about the journey of learning, experimenting, and growing. He once said, "The most certain way to succeed is always to try just one more time." This sentiment underscores the importance of perseverance and resilience and reinforces that effort and personal growth are integral parts of success.

As we reflect on Edison's life, it's clear that his growth mindset was a contributor to his many accomplishments. We can glean valuable insights from his attitude toward challenges, his commitment to learning, his resilience in the face of adversity, and his unique definition of success. Incorporating these learnings into our own lives can help us cultivate a growth mindset and empower us to overcome obstacles and achieve our own versions of success.

Embracing the Journey of Growth

The path to growth requires you to adopt a holistic approach that encompasses self-awareness, continuous learning, and self-compassion. Each of these elements contributes to nurturing a growth mindset. Remember, the path may be challenging, but the rewards are fulfilling. Be patient and persistent, and above all, always keep an open mind to discovering your limitless potential.

Reinforcing a Mindset Shift Through Reflection

A significant part of transitioning to a growth mindset involves recognizing your thoughts and attitudes toward abilities, challenges, and failures. An effective way to facilitate this transition is by maintaining a journal dedicated to your mindset. By noting down your thoughts and reactions to different situations, you'll gain a clearer understanding of your current mindset and monitor its evolution toward growth.

Consider this scenario: You've been tasked with a project at work that requires skills you haven't fully developed. Document your initial reactions, your feelings throughout the project, and your observations after completing the task. This exercise can provide valuable insights into your mindset.

Celebrating Progress in the Journey

In fostering a growth mindset, every improvement counts, no matter how small. Recognizing and celebrating your progress affirms the belief that abilities can be developed. This celebration can be a moment of self-acknowledgment and doesn't necessarily need an elaborate affair.

Perhaps you've taken on a challenging project, and you've successfully completed it. Take a moment to celebrate this victory—treat yourself to your favorite dessert, share the accomplishment with a friend, or simply take a moment to acknowledge your progress.

Taking Inspiration From Others' Journeys

The practice of appreciating others' journeys involves understanding their effort, persistence, and learning. Not only does this give you inspiration, but it also reinforces your understanding of the growth mindset in action.

For example, read autobiographies of successful individuals in your field of interest. Pay attention to their struggles and their attitude toward challenges and failures.

Nelson Mandela's life journey, as chronicled in his autobiography *Long Walk to Freedom*, can provide numerous lessons on the growth mindset. Here are five key takeaways condensed with corresponding journal prompts:

1. Embracing Challenges: Mandela faced immense adversity with fortitude.

Journal Prompt: Reflect on a major challenge in your life. How did you react to it, and how can you use Mandela's example to better embrace such situations in the future?

2. Persistence in the Face of Setbacks: Mandela didn't let setbacks deter him from his ultimate goal of a free and equal South Africa.

Journal Prompt: Write about a time you faced a setback. How did you handle it then, and how might you apply Mandela's perseverance to similar situations moving forward?

3. Lifelong Learning: Mandela committed himself to continuous learning and growth.

Journal Prompt: Identify a new skill or area of knowledge you want to explore. How can you commit to being a lifelong learner like Mandela?

4. Vision for the Future: Mandela held a strong vision for the future, even when it seemed far-fetched.

Journal Prompt: Write about your vision for your future. How can you hold onto this vision during challenging times?

5. Redefining Success: Mandela viewed success not as personal gain, but as achieving freedom for his country.

Journal Prompt: Reflect on your definition of success. How does it align with Mandela's perspective, and what changes, if any, would you like to make?

Remember, the goal of these journal prompts is to inspire introspection and growth.

Embracing Continuous Learning

Learning doesn't have to involve monumental tasks. Small steps toward expanding your knowledge and skills can significantly impact your mindset.

Try adopting a new hobby, learning a new recipe, or reading a book outside your usual genre. These seemingly small steps can cumulatively contribute to the development of a growth mindset.

Learning From Mistakes

In the context of a growth mindset, mistakes become teachers, providing valuable lessons. This perspective encourages risk-taking and fosters growth.

The next time you make a mistake, instead of dwelling on the error, reflect on the lessons it offers. What could you do differently next time? What has this experience taught you?

Practicing Self-Compassion

Growth is a journey with its own set of challenges and setbacks. Self-compassion is a crucial ally during this journey, providing a safe space for growth and learning.

When you next face a setback, instead of beating yourself up, offer yourself the same kindness you would to a friend. Remind yourself that setbacks are a part of growth, and it's okay to falter sometimes.

Utilizing Examples for Motivation

Examples, whether from your own life or from that of others, can serve as powerful motivation to embrace a growth mindset. These real-life instances act as proof of the power and potential of adopting a growth mindset.

Reflect on a time when you overcame a challenge by maintaining a growth mindset. Alternatively, consider famous personalities known for their growth mindset like Michael Jordan or Oprah Winfrey.

Setting SMART Goals for Growth

SMART goals provide a clear direction for your growth journey. They also allow for easier tracking of progress and sustained motivation.

Instead of having a broad goal such as "I want to write better," aim for a SMART goal like "I will write for 30 minutes every day for the next three months to improve my writing skills."

As you continue integrating these steps into your daily life, you'll notice a transformative shift in your mindset and approach toward abilities, challenges, and failures. The path toward a growth mindset might not always be easy, but the rewards it reaps—in resilience, openness to learning, and acceptance of mistakes—are profoundly enriching. With patience, persistence, and abundant self-compassion, your journey toward a growth mindset will unveil your untapped potential.

7D. INTERACTIVE ELEMENT

Harnessing the Power of Active Participation

Journaling isn't simply an exercise in writing; it's an active engagement with your thought process. By recording your experiences, thoughts, and feelings, you move beyond passive learning. This interactive method urges you to process your ideas and scrutinize them, a practice that is instrumental in fostering a growth mindset.

Consider a situation where you were presented with a major challenge. How did you handle it? What was the outcome? Such questions prompt an assessment of your mindset in addressing challenges, thereby revealing if you're rooted in a fixed or growth mindset.

Transforming fixed-mindset beliefs

Journaling allows you to face your fixed-mindset beliefs head-on. Imagine a skill or task that you currently believe is beyond your capabilities. How would your perspective shift if you added 'yet' to that belief? By posing questions like this, you facilitate the transition from a fixed mindset to one of growth.

For example:

- Fixed mindset: "I can't play the guitar."
- Growth mindset: "I can't play the guitar yet."

Highlighting Progress and Achievement

Journaling about accomplishments, regardless of size, strengthens the idea that abilities can be developed. Moreover, reflecting on the lessons you've learned from missteps nurtures a healthier perspective toward failure, which, in turn, emboldens you to take risks.

Try jotting down some of your recent achievements. No success is too small.

Setting Goals and Tracking Progress

Writing down your SMART goals in your journal helps reinforce your faith in your capacity to evolve. Regularly tracking your progress toward these goals solidifies this belief further.

For instance, you might set goals as such:

- Specific: "I want to improve my public speaking skills."
- Measurable: "I will join a local Toastmasters club and participate in meetings."
- Achievable: "I will give at least one speech every month."
- Relevant: "This will help me to improve my communication skills for work."

- Time-bound: "I will achieve this goal within a year."

Nurturing Self-Compassion

Self-compassion prompts also play a crucial role. They encourage you to write affirmations or kind notes to yourself during times of struggle or failure. This practice not only nurtures a healthier response to setbacks but also encourages a growth mindset.

Reframing Failure

Reevaluating your understanding of failure is a key aspect of cultivating a growth mindset. Reflect on a recent setback or failure. How did it affect your subsequent actions? Could you have harnessed it as a learning opportunity instead? Such introspection aids in repurposing failure from a negative event to an opportunity for growth.

Celebrating the Journey

Learning to appreciate the journey, not just the destination, is vital for a growth mindset. Write about a goal you've recently accomplished. Focus not on the end result, but on significant moments of growth and learning throughout your journey.

The Power of Positive Affirmations and Self-Compassion

Lastly, embrace the impact of positive affirmations and self-compassion. Recall a moment when you were overly critical of yourself. What would you have told a friend in the same situation? How can you extend this compassion to yourself?

A well-structured catalog of journal prompts promoting introspection and a growth mindset can be a powerful tool for personal development. Each prompt aims to guide you into deeper self-reflection, challenging you to reassess your current mindset and gradually transition toward a growth mindset.

Exploring Growth Mindset Examples

To solidify your belief in the potential of a growth mindset, reflect on real-life examples. These could be personal experiences or incidents involving others where a growth mindset was clearly exhibited. Illustrating this in your journal can further strengthen your belief in the ability to change and grow.

For instance, remember a time when you initially struggled with a new task, like learning a foreign language or a complex mathematical concept, but gradually improved with consistent effort and practice. Reflect on how this growth happened and how it affected your mindset.

Challenging Adversity With a Growth Mindset

Identifying your natural tendencies in the face of adversity is crucial for personal growth. Consider a situation where you were faced with a significant challenge. Did you shy away from it, fearing potential failure, or did you embrace it as an opportunity for growth and learning?

Asking questions like, "Moving forward, how can I ensure to approach similar challenges with a growth mindset?" can help pave the way for personal transformation.

Unpacking the "I Can't Do This Yet" Perspective

Taking the time to unpack the "I can't do this yet" perspective can be extremely rewarding. It transforms challenges from being perceived as insurmountable obstacles into opportunities for learning and growth. Reflect on something you've always wanted to learn or achieve but didn't because you felt intimidated by the prospect. How might your perspective change if you shifted from a mindset of "I can't do this" to "I can't do this yet"?

For example, if you've always wanted to write a book but felt overwhelmed by the task, changing your perspective to "I can't write a book yet" can provide the encouragement you need to take the first step.

Promoting Self-Compassion

Finally, employing positive affirmations and self-compassion can foster a growth mindset. Reflect on a recent occasion when you were particularly hard on yourself. This exercise teaches you to be more forgiving toward yourself.

Suggested Prompts

1. Write about a time when you faced a significant challenge. How did you handle it? What did you learn from it?
2. Reflect on your strengths. How do these strengths help you navigate through difficulties?
3. Identify a failure or setback that happened recently. What can you learn from this experience? How can this help you grow?

4. Write about a skill you would like to master. What steps can you take to achieve this?

5. Reflect on criticism or feedback you received recently. How can you use them for your personal growth?

6. Imagine yourself five years from now. What personal growth would you like to see?

7. How can you incorporate perseverance into your daily habits?

8. Identify three ways you can step out of your comfort zone this week.

9. How does the concept of "effort leading to mastery" resonate with you?

10. Describe a time when you witnessed growth in yourself that you didn't think was possible.

11. Write about how your perception of failure has evolved over time.

12. What motivates you to keep going when things get tough?

13. How can you turn your weaknesses into opportunities for growth?

14. Write about a recent experience that made you feel out of place or uncomfortable. How can this contribute to your personal growth?

15. Reflect on a time when you demonstrated resilience. How can you further cultivate this trait?

16. Write about an area in your life where you can embrace more growth and less perfection.

17. What new habits can you adopt to promote a growth mindset?

18. Write about a goal that seems impossible now. What would be the first step toward achieving it?

19. Reflect on a time you made a mistake. How did it contribute to your growth?

20. How do you define success? Does this definition promote a growth mindset?

Summing Up

By integrating these prompts into your journaling practice, you're doing more than simply documenting your experiences; you're creating a potent resource for personal growth and development. Each entry provides a snapshot of your mindset at a particular moment, offering insights into your progress toward a growth mindset over time. This interactive tool encourages you to grapple with your current mindset and gently nudge yourself toward embracing a growth mindset, all while providing an ongoing record of your journey.

7E. KEY TAKEAWAYS

We looked into the transformative power of culti-vating a growth mindset in this chapter, revealing how it can promote personal and professional devel-opment. In contrast to the fixed mindset, the growth mindset allows us to push past self-imposed bound-aries and overcome limiting beliefs.

- We emphasized the numerous advantages of adopting a growth mindset, such as fostering personal growth and resilience.
- We saw how a growth mindset directly fuels resilience, preparing us to face adversity, learn from failures, and bounce back stronger, using practical examples. This mindset gives us the tools we need to challenge and change our limiting beliefs, propelling us to our full potential.
- Thomas Edison's inspirational story demonstrates the power of a growth mindset. Despite thousands of failed attempts to create the electric light bulb,

Edison's unwavering confidence in his ability to succeed exemplified the growth mindset. His view of failure as a learning opportunity rather than evidence of incompetence reinforces the core essence of a growth mindset.

A growth mindset is more than just believing in the possibility of change. It is about accepting failure, persevering through difficulties, and viewing every setback as a chance for learning and growth. This powerful mindset has the potential to be a catalyst in our personal transformation and success.

An Opportunity to Inspire Someone Else

As you set forth on this exciting journey, you're in the perfect position to guide someone else along theirs.

Simply by sharing your honest opinion of this book and a little about your own experience, you'll show new readers how they can unlock this adventure of growth and self-discovery for themselves.

WANT TO HELP OTHERS?

Thank you so much for your support. I'm excited for everything that lies ahead of you.

Scan the QR code to leave a review!

CONCLUSION

We have journeyed through the corridors of self-doubt, traversed the landscapes of self-perception, and delved into the labyrinth of limiting beliefs. We have peered into the mirror of self-awareness, and hopefully, emerged with an empowered sense of self.

Through the course of this book, we have

- engaged in critical discussions around the power and impact of our mindset.
- dissected the difference between a fixed mindset and a growth mindset, highlighting the pivotal role the latter plays in the pursuit of our personal and professional goals.

- explored the stifling influence of limiting beliefs and the liberating potential of empowering beliefs.
- examined the concept of resilience and its relationship with a growth mindset, shedding light on how they work in tandem to combat self-doubt and pave the way to success.

Each chapter in this book is a testament to the power of transformation, an affirmation of the potential that lies within each one of us. One key takeaway is that no barrier is too high, no obstacle too daunting, if you believe in your ability to overcome them. By cultivating a growth mindset, you can redefine your reality, transform your outlook, and step into a world of limitless possibilities.

The journey of self-discovery is not linear. It is fraught with challenges and setbacks, but it is equally filled with triumphs and breakthroughs. Allow me to share a personal success story that reinforces the lessons we have learned throughout this book.

Do you remember the anecdote I shared from my childhood about my art teacher's casual remark that sparked a series of limiting beliefs in me? Years later, after I had navigated through my doubts and fears and challenged my limiting beliefs and negative self-talk, I found myself standing before a blank canvas, paintbrush in hand. I was hesitant at first, the old self-doubt creeping in like an unwelcome guest. But as I let the paintbrush dance on the canvas, a familiar sense of joy and fulfillment washed over me. It wasn't about being good enough for someone else's approval; it was about expressing myself, my thoughts, my emotions, and finding happiness in the process. Today, not only do I continue to paint for my own enjoyment, but I've also incorporated art and creative expression into my life coaching practice. It serves as a testament to the transformative power of challenging your limiting beliefs and adopting a growth mindset.

With the wisdom gleaned from this book, you are now equipped to combat your limiting beliefs. It is your turn to take up the paintbrush of your life, so to speak, and paint the canvas of your dreams. Set your goals, outline a plan, and take that first step toward the life you desire and deserve.

The journey to personal growth and success is continuous, at least it doesn't end with the last page of this book. Keep practicing the techniques you have learned here. Keep questioning, keep growing, keep believing in yourself. With determination, perseverance, and an unwavering belief in your abilities, believe that you can overcome any obstacle and live a fulfilling life that extends beyond your wildest dreams.

If this book has made a difference in your journey, please consider leaving a review. Your feedback not only helps me understand your perspective, but it also enables others to discover this guide. Remember, our stories and experiences can empower and inspire others in their journey toward personal growth and success.

So, dear reader, go ahead. The canvas of your life awaits your unique colors. Unleash the power of your potential and paint a masterpiece beyond comparison. Your journey to personal growth, success, and fulfillment begins now. You have the power to shape your destiny and live your dreams. Believe in your abilities, embrace the potential of a growth mindset, and unlock the door to a world of endless possibilities.

REFERENCES

Amabile, T., & Kramer, S. (2011). *The progress principle: Using small wins to ignite joy, engagement, and creativity at work.* Harvard Business Review Press.

American Psychological Association. (2021, October). *Stress and decision-making during the pandemic: Stress in America 2021.* American Psychological Association. https://www.apa.org/news/press/releases/stress/2021/october-decision-making

Arnsten, A. F. (2009). Stress signalling pathways that impair prefrontal cortex structure and function. *Nature Reviews Neuroscience, 10*(6), 410-422. https://doi.org/10.1038/nrn2648

Baumeister, R. F., Bratslavsky, E., Finkenauer, C., & Vohs, K. D. (2001). Bad is stronger than good. *Review of General Psychology, 5*(4), 323-370. https://doi.org/10.1037/1089-2680.5.4.323

Burns, R. A., & Anstey, K. J. (2010). The Connor–Davidson Resilience Scale (CD-RISC): Testing the invariance of a unidimensional resilience measure that is independent of positive and negative affect. *Personality and Individual Differences, 48*(5), 527-531.

Chen, S., Westman, M., & Hobfoll, S. E. (2015). The commerce and crossover of resources: Resource conservation in the service of resilience. *Stress and Health, 31*(2), 95-105. https://doi.org/10.1002/smi.2574

Cleveland Clinic. (2021, June 24). *How to practice mindfulness to improve your well-being.* Cleveland Clinic. https://health.clevelandclinic.org/practice-mindfulness-to-improve-your-well-being-11-tips/

Clough, P., Earle, K., & Sewell, D. (2002). Mental toughness: The concept and its measurement. In I. Cockerill (Ed.), *Solutions in sport psychology* (pp. 32-43). Thomson.

Connor, K. M., & Davidson, J. R. (2003). Development of a new resilience scale: The Connor-Davidson Resilience Scale (CD-RISC). *Depression and Anxiety, 18*(2), 76-82.

Crust, L., & Azadi, K. (2010). Mental toughness and athletes' use of psychological strategies. *European Journal of Sport Science, 10*(1), 43-51.

Crust, L., & Clough, P. J. (2005). Relationship between mental toughness and physical endurance. *Perceptual and Motor Skills, 100*(1), 192-194. https://doi.org/10.2466/PMS.100.1.192-194

Cumming, J., & Williams, S. E. (2012). The role of imagery in performance. Handbook of sport and performance psychology, 213-232.

Cuncic, A. (2020, June 29). *How to stop negative thoughts*. Verywell Mind. https://www.verywellmind.com/how-to-change-negative-thinking-3024843

Damasio, A. R. (1994). *Descartes' error: Emotion, reason, and the human brain*. Putnam.

Davidson, R. J., & McEwen, B. S. (2012). Social influences on neuroplasticity: stress and interventions to promote well-being. *Nature Neuroscience, 15*(5), 689-695. https://doi.org/10.1038/nn.3093

Dayan, E., & Cohen, L. G. (2011). Neuroplasticity subserving motor skill learning. *Neuron, 72*(3), 443-454. https://doi.org/10.1016/j.neuron.2011.10.008

Doran, G. T. (1981). There's a S.M.A.R.T. way to write management's goals and objectives. *Management Review, 70*(11), 35-36.

Duckworth, A. L. (2016). Grit: *The power of passion and perseverance*. Simon and Schuster.

Dweck, C. (2006). *Mindset: The new psychology of success.* Random House.

Ellis, A. (1991). The revised ABC's of rational-emotive therapy (RET). *Journal of Rational-Emotive and Cognitive-Behavior Therapy, 9*(3), 139-172.

Emmons, R. A., & McCullough, M. E. (2003). Counting blessings versus burdens: an experimental investigation of gratitude and subjective well-being in daily life. *Journal of Personality and Social Psychology, 84*(2), 377-389.

Fredrickson, B. L. (2001). The role of positive emotions in positive psychology: The broaden-and-build theory of positive emotions. *American psychologist, 56*(3), 218-226.

Goleman, D. (1995). *Emotional intelligence.* Bantam Books.

Gomez-Pinilla, F., & Hillman, C. (2013). The Influence of Exercise on Cognitive Abilities. *Comprehensive Physiology, 3*(1), 403-428. https://doi.org/10.1002/cphy.c110063

Grider, H. S., Douglas, S. M., & Raynor, H. A. (2020). The Influence of Mindful Eating and/or Intuitive Eating Approaches on Dietary Intake: A Systematic Review. *Journal of the Academy of Nutrition and Dietetics, 121*(4). https://doi.org/10.1016/j.jand.2020.10.019

Gross, J. J. (1998). The emerging field of emotion regulation: An integrative review. *Review of General Psychology, 2*(3), 271-299.

Gross, J. J., & John, O. P. (2003). Individual differences in two emotion regulation processes: Implications for affect, relationships, and well-being. *Journal of Personality and Social Psychology, 85*(2), 348-362.

Gross, J. J., & Thompson, R. A. (2007). Emotion regulation: Conceptual foundations. In J. J. Gross (Ed.), *Handbook of emotion regulation* (pp. 3-24). The Guilford Press.

Gucciardi, D. F., Hanton, S., & Mallett, C. J. (2012). Progressing measurement in mental toughness: A case study of the

Mental Toughness Questionnaire 48. *Sport, Exercise, and Performance Psychology, 1*(3), 194-214.

Hölzel, B. K., Carmody, J., Vangel, M., Congleton, C., Yerramsetti, S. M., Gard, T., & Lazar, S. W. (2011). Mindfulness practice leads to increases in regional brain gray matter density. *Psychiatry Research: Neuroimaging, 191*(1), 36-43. https://doi.org/10.1016/j.pscychresns.2010.08.006

Hudson, N. W., & Fraley, R. C. (2015). Volitional personality trait change: Can people choose to change their personality traits? *Journal of Personality and Social Psychology, 109*(3), 490-507. Jones, G., Hanton, S., & Connaughton, D. (2007). A framework of mental toughness in the world's best performers. *The Sport Psychologist, 21*(2), 243-264.

Kabat-Zinn, J. (1994). *Wherever you go, there you are: Mindfulness meditation in everyday life*. Hyperion.

Kim, E. J., Pellman, B., & Kim, J. J. (2015). Stress effects on the hippocampus: a critical review. *Learning & Memory, 22*(9), 411-416. https://dx.doi.org/10.1101/lm.037291.114

Laborde, S., Dosseville, F., & Allen, M. S. (2016). Emotional intelligence in sport and exercise: A systematic review. *Scandinavian Journal of Medicine & Science in Sports, 26*(8), 862-874.

Lazarus, R. S., & Folkman, S. (1984). *Stress, Appraisal, and Coping*. Springer Publishing Company.

LeDoux, J. (1996). *The emotional brain: The mysterious underpinnings of emotional life*. Simon and Schuster.

Lyubomirsky, S., & Layous, K. (2013). How do simple positive activities increase well-being? *Current Directions in Psychological Science, 22*(1), 57-62.

Maddi, S. R. (2006). Hardiness: The courage to grow from stresses. *Journal of Positive Psychology, 1*(3), 160-168.

Mayer, J. D., & Salovey, P. (1997). What is emotional intelligence? In P. Salovey & D. J. Sluyter (Eds.), *Emotional develop-*

ment and emotional intelligence: Educational implications (pp. 3-31). Basic Books.

Miller, G. A., Galanter, E., & Pribram, K. H. (1960). *Plans and the structure of behavior*. Holt, Rinehart, and Winston.

Mischel, W., & Shoda, Y. (2008). Toward a unified theory of personality: Integrating dispositions and processing dynamics within the cognitive-affective processing system. In O. P. John, R. W. Robins, & L. A. Pervin (Eds.), *Handbook of personality: Theory and research* (pp. 208-241). The Guilford Press.

Morawetz, C., Bode, S., Baudewig, J., & Heekeren, H. R. (2016). Effective amygdala-prefrontal connectivity predicts individual differences in successful emotion regulation. *Social Cognitive and Affective Neuroscience, 12*(4), 569-585. https://doi.org/10.1093/scan/nsw169

Mõttus, R., Kandler, C., Bleidorn, W., Riemann, R., & McCrae, R. R. (2017). Personality traits below facets: The consensual validity, longitudinal stability, heritability, and utility of personality nuances. *Journal of Personality and Social Psychology, 112*(3), 474-490. https://doi.org/10.1037/pspp0000100

Niemiec, C. P., & Ryan, R. M. (2009). Autonomy, competence, and relatedness in the classroom: Applying self-determination theory to educational practice. *Theory and Research in Education, 7*(2), 133-144.

Ochsner, K. N., & Gross, J. J. (2005). The cognitive control of emotion. *Trends in Cognitive Sciences, 9*(5), 242-249.

Park, N., Peterson, C., & Seligman, M. E. (2004). Strengths of character and well-being. *Journal of Social and Clinical Psychology, 23*(5), 603-619.

Ryff, C. D., & Keyes, C. L. (1995). The structure of psychological well-being revisited. *Journal of Personality and Social Psychology, 69*(4), 719-727.

Seligman, M. E. (2011). *Flourish: A visionary new understanding of happiness and well-being*. Simon and Schuster.

Selye, H. (1956). *The stress of life*. McGraw-Hill.

Siddle, J., Greig, M., Weaver, K., Page, R. M., Harper, D., & Brogden, C. M. (2018). Acute adaptations and subsequent preservation of strength and speed measures following a Nordic hamstring curl intervention: a randomised controlled trial. *Journal of Sports Sciences, 37*(8), 911-920. https://doi.org/10.1080/02640414.2018.1535786

Simone, F. (2017, December 4). *Negative self-talk: Don't let it overwhelm you*. Psychology Today. https://www.psychologytoday.com/us/blog/family-affair/201712/negative-self-talk-dont-let-it-overwhelm-you

Snyder, C. R., & Lopez, S. J. (2009). *Oxford handbook of positive psychology*. Oxford University Press.

Spinelli, C., Wisener, M., & Khoury, B. (2019). Mindfulness training for healthcare professionals and trainees: A meta-analysis of randomized controlled trials. *Journal of Psychosomatic Research, 120*, 29-38. https://doi.org/10.1016/j.jpsychores.2019.03.003

Steptoe, A., Deaton, A., & Stone, A. A. (2015). Subjective wellbeing, health, and ageing. *The Lancet, 385*(9968), 640-648.

Street, P., White, D., & Netlibrary, I. (2002). *Picabo: Nothing to hide*. Contemporary Books.

Tang, Y.-Y., Hölzel, B. K., & Posner, M. I. (2015). The neuroscience of mindfulness meditation. *Nature Reviews Neuroscience, 16*(4), 213-225. https://doi.org/10.1038/nrn3916

Top 25 limiting beliefs quotes. (n.d.). A-Z Quotes. https://www.azquotes.com/quotes/topics/limiting-beliefs.html

Tugade, M. M., & Fredrickson, B. L. (2004). Resilient individuals use positive emotions to bounce back from negative emotional experiences. *Journal of Personality and Social Psychology, 86*(2), 320-333.

Watson, D., & Clark, L. A. (1994). *The PANAS-X: Manual for the positive and negative affect schedule-expanded form.* University of Iowa.

Watts, A. W., Rydell, S. A., Eisenberg, M. E., Laska, M. N., & Neumark-Sztainer, D. (2018). Yoga's potential for promoting healthy eating and physical activity behaviors among young adults: a mixed-methods study. *International Journal of Behavioral Nutrition and Physical Activity, 15*(1). https://doi.org/10.1186/s12966-018-0674-4

Wilding, M. (2021, February 10). *How to stop overthinking everything.* Harvard Business Review. https://hbr.org/2021/02/how-to-stop-overthinking-everything

Wood, A. M., Joseph, S., & Maltby, J. (2008). Gratitude uniquely predicts satisfaction with life: Incremental validity above the domains and facets of the Five Factors. *Personality and Individual Differences, 45*(1), 49-54.

Woodman, T., Davis, P. A., Hardy, L., Callow, N., & Glasscock, I. (2009). Emotion regulation in sport: An individualized approach to emotional challenges in elite and non-elite athletes. *International Journal of Sport and Exercise Psychology, 7*(3), 259-273.

Made in the USA
Las Vegas, NV
22 January 2024

84723001R00118